Teaching *Huckleberry Finn*

ALSO BY JOHN NOGOWSKI

Bob Dylan: A Descriptive, Critical Discography and Filmography, 1961–2007, 2d ed. (McFarland, 2008)

Teaching Huckleberry Finn

Why and How to Present the Controversial Classic in the High School Classroom

John Nogowski

McFarland & Company, Inc., Publishers
Jefferson, North Carolina

LIBRARY OF CONGRESS CATALOGUING-IN-PUBLICATION DATA

Names: Nogowski, John, 1953– author.
Title: Teaching Huckleberry Finn : why and how to present the controversial classic in the high school classroom / John Nogowski.
Description: Jefferson, North Carolina : McFarland & Company, Inc., Publishers, 2018. | Includes bibliographical references and index.
Identifiers: LCCN 2018027538 | ISBN 9781476674285 (softcover : acid free paper) ♾
Subjects: LCSH: Twain, Mark, 1835–1910. Adventures of Huckleberry Finn. | Twain, Mark, 1835–1910—Study and teaching. | Literature and society—United States—History—19th century. | Finn, Huckleberry (Fictitious character) | Prohibited books—United States.
Classification: LCC PS1305 .N57 2018 | DDC 813/.4—dc23
LC record available at https://lccn.loc.gov/2018027538

BRITISH LIBRARY CATALOGUING DATA ARE AVAILABLE

ISBN (print) 978-1-4766-7428-5
ISBN (ebook) 978-1-4766-3307-7

© 2018 John Nogowski. All rights reserved

No part of this book may be reproduced or transmitted in any form or by any means, electronic or mechanical, including photocopying or recording, or by any information storage and retrieval system, without permission in writing from the publisher.

Front cover image frontispiece in: *Adventures of Huckleberry Finn* by Mark Twain. New York, Charles L. Webster and Co., 1884 (Library of Congress); *background* painting of trees beside the river © 2018 Max5799/iStock

Printed in the United States of America

McFarland & Company, Inc., Publishers
  Box 611, Jefferson, North Carolina 28640
  www.mcfarlandpub.com

Dedications—

Best Teacher: *To Sister Lorraine Trottier, who helped a high school jock stranded in a Catholic girls' college (really) to learn to think and write and grow and find a career. Thank you, Sister; you did it with patience (remember my 111–page term paper?), wisdom and love. And you sat through game six of the 1975 World Series (Fisk's walk-off HR!). God bless you!*

Best Boss: *To Mike Connell, an editor who gave me a chance when it seemed no one would; then encouraged, nudged and guided me through four extraordinary, award-winning years in Port Huron. You changed my life and my career. Thank you, forever ... my friend.*

Best Friend: *To Mark Fountain, who helped get me started with Mr. Twain when we were kids many years ago. One of my great personal thrills was surprising you in Boston as we took you to see Hal Holbrook in* Mark Twain Tonight *for the first time. You've been a wonderful friend, someone I could always count on, and someone who was always there, ready to help. You're the best.*

Table of Contents

Preface   1

Introduction: Why Huck? Why Now?   3

1. Wrestling with the "N" Word   15
2. A Rich Tapestry of Themes   25
3. A Splash, a Split and a Pause   38
4. Twain Stops the Show—As Intended   46
5. Navigating His Way to the Finish   52
6. A Critical Casserole—Who's Right?   62
7. Incorrect Correctness, Another Flawed Finish   75

Appendix A: Two Critical Responses to Huckleberry Finn   83

Appendix B: Selected Short Works by Twain, with Annotations   105

Appendix C: Additional Twain-Related Assignments   150

Suggested Reading and Viewing   154

Index   169

Preface

Writing a preface for *Teaching* Huckleberry Finn was not something I initially thought about. Just never came up. I've written an introduction but not a preface. But since a preface sets the tone, why not? First off, my scholarship might not be termed academically mainstream; I'm a 60-plus-year-old reformed sportswriter who teaches African-American students in what has been a traditionally failing school. It is about as far away from the Ivy League as you can get. When it comes to the content—that is, talking about how Twain's classic novel applies to today's high school students and their lives—I don't think it could be any *more* mainstream. And to my way of thinking, that's very valuable.

As anyone who's ever taught knows that it's one thing to write critical theory; it's another to put your ideas and concepts into practice for a bunch of impressionable students. For me, *Teaching* Huckleberry Finn is the product of seven years on the front line of high school teaching and a lifetime of reading the work of maybe our most important author, Mark Twain.

There are those who would strongly disagree with that assessment. Like, say, Jane Smiley, whose criticisms I will address later on. It's agreed that Jane Smiley, an accomplished, well-respected novelist of note, has a considerable literary reputation. I have none. It is entirely possible that her vastly superior education, her grasp of fiction and professional success, will leave me in the literary dust. Yet after spending all this time with Twain's work and seeing the impact it has had and continues to have on young audiences, her critique and what is in my view a complete misunderstanding of the significance of Twain's work leaves me breathless. Not speechless.

Over the years of teaching and discussing and debating and reading everything available regarding Twain and this book, I am more convinced

Preface

than ever of its value, whatever its flaws, especially in these fractious, divisive times. There may be no better book for us, certainly for our young people, to read and discuss.

I am not sure I would call myself a scholar, yet I doubt there are many educators in America who have taken Twain's work, *Huckleberry Finn*, in particular, into the places I have and come out on the other side. No, my interest in *Huck* is of a more practical nature.

In my role as an educator, there's so much more that goes into teaching than just relating to or memorizing or dissecting a text. Particularly in a school like mine where often, I'll be teaching a student or three who have never read a single book before. So, if you're going to try and introduce this young person to literature, to something that will stay with them forever, you ought to pick carefully.

Over the hours and days and years, wading through the student papers, measuring the in-class comments and discussions, this is a look at Twain's work from the ground up, at the moments that touched them, enlightened them and for some, I really think it helped change their life (the names used in the book are pseudonyms).

In the current political climate, one that's hit my school as well, I'm fearful that books that challenge us like *Huckleberry Finn*—books that are or can be difficult or controversial will just be abandoned for fear of that controversy, the idea of upsetting some mom or some well-meaning, ill-informed school board member. Don't teach the best stuff, teach the least offensive, things no one will object to—or remember.

Despite seven successful years teaching *Huckleberry Finn*, the administrators at my school, sadly, mirroring the reaction of many other administrators across this land, didn't even want to discuss it when this school year rolled around. After an incident last year that will be discussed later, they were steering clear of the topic.

"Let's don't even bring it up," one said, firmly.

For all these reasons, I think the lessons and stories that came from these years of teaching Twain's work (not just *Huck*) are worth examining, reconsidering how and why we teach and what we hope to achieve. In compiling this book, looking back at student papers, classroom discussions, email exchanges with other teachers, reading just about every Twain and *Huckleberry Finn* commentary around, I wanted to share some of what I've learned with other teachers and readers and friends I haven't met yet.

Introduction:
Why *Huck*? Why Now?

I thought of one word: help. What if the books could talk back? What could they tell me?

It was an early August morning and I stood there all alone in my school's book room, a steamy, out-of-the-way little hole in the gray cement wall, next door to the cafeteria; a generally neglected storage location cluttered with books and workbooks from all corners of the academic spectrum. For veteran teachers, a visit here is a boring annual rite of passage—oh, yes, I'll need a classroom set of *The Great Gatsby* and *The Crucible* and, let's see, *A Raisin in the Sun* and *To Kill a Mockingbird*. You know, the usual fare.

As a new teacher, at least new to high school environs, I wondered if there were words in these books that could help me. Ostensibly, I was there to select my textbooks for the upcoming academic year, which would start in a couple weeks. Being ambitious, idealistic and, yes, unbelievably naïve, I hoped for more. Though I hadn't yet taught a single class here at what was then East Gadsden High School, I already had a pretty good idea of what I would be up against.

A recent story that appeared on the website *Salon* laid out the situation pretty well: "Though (Gadsden County) it's still home to a handful of Coca-Cola stock-owning millionaires, the median household income is $36,000, about a quarter less than the statewide average.... Gadsden has the largest percentage of black students of any traditional school district in Florida. Nearly three-quarters of its students are black (a higher percentage at my school), just under 20 percent are Latino and fewer than 4 percent are white. Three-quarters are considered economically disadvantaged by the state." With 100 percent of the school on free or reduced

Introduction

lunch, a long-running series of sub-par grades from the state of Florida, and ever-changing administrators, this may be the Mariana Trench of Florida high school academics.

Okay, so it's not optimum teaching ground; we get that. Considering that less than 15 percent of the student body can read and perform at grade level (a recent test placed my 10th graders at 4.65 grade level), understanding that teacher retention (6 of 8 from last year gone) is perpetually an issue and student attendance (or lack of it) seem to be never-ending problems, you understand what I was facing. Any educator starting here is in for a real challenge. Given all this, it was immediately clear to me that the Florida Department of Education's recommended techniques would not work in an environment like this. I couldn't just pick a textbook and pop out a lesson plan like at any other school.

If I was going to make a difference here, I wanted something that would shake up their world, a bomb. If I could find it, I wanted an assortment of words and themes and ideas that would find a way into their heads and toss things around. I needed something radical, something earth-shaking. So ... when I looked over in a corner and saw pristine copies of a famous, if controversial book that, the more I looked at it, seemed to be seething. Why, here's *The Adventures of Huckleberry Finn*, a whole stack of 'em, looking like they were being quarantined. I moved closer and got to thinking...

It is quite a sight to stand there in the bookroom after a school year. These textbooks had been in the daily line of battle, and now they were trying to get over the battle scars of a year in the open classroom. You know those scars; maybe you added to them back in your day. You remember those kids who couldn't just leave the book alone. Writing on the side of the page, tearing out a page, scribbling in the margins, anything to deface it.

Staring at these battered books, so much for immortality. Yeah, they might have been classics in their day, but they were a long way from a time where they were celebrated by one and all. Long gone were the magical days where the beauty and wisdom and eloquence strewn across those glittering pages made the experience of just holding it in your hands lift one up ... well, they were forgotten. What would ol' Harper Lee think of some kid writing a curse word on the edges of her *To Kill a Mockingbird?* Imagine the sour look on F. Scott Fitzgerald's face if he saw a couple of his perfectly crafted pages of *The Great Gatsby* ripped out to throw at a class-

Why Huck? Why Now?

mate? If you care about books, about writing, it was like being in a hospital ward.

But *Huck*? Here, in pristine shape, neatly stacked in a corner, were 30 yellow and white copies of Mark Twain's *The Adventures of Huckleberry Finn*. They looked pissed. For a moment, I let myself imagine how those 30 copies of *Huck* felt, watching all these *other* books trotted off to classrooms all over campus while they had to sit in darkness for months at a time. Twain spent seven tortuous years on this book, trying to find the right way to make America confront its built-in racism, and yet, here it was, in a place where it could make an impact and it was sitting here, steaming. Why, I half-expected Twain's book to start talking to me once I picked it up.

Huck was neglected as a child and, well, here it was, happening again. Sure, Twain's book was still taught around the country in lots of schools, still stirring up trouble, but it had never been taught here. Sequestered away in a book room of a traditionally failing school in a county that could not seem to dig itself out of a recurring academic nightmare, the book that might have better connected with its students than any other scared most teachers off.

I could see their concerns. It is not an easy book to teach. Not only is *Huck* a book that was written over 100 years ago, there were just too many issues: dialect, hearing that poisonous "N" word in class every day, it's just too long. What about having to explain—and revisit—slavery? The humor, would that still work? And in my case, what about having an older white teacher read a book with the "N" word in it? In class every day? How would my black students handle that?

It was something to think about. I didn't make my choice just then. I walked back to my classroom and on the way, got a pretty good idea why the book was ignored. Next door to me, an African-American woman was writing on the board. We chatted for a bit. She asked what novel I was going to teach and I mentioned *Huck Finn*. She looked stunned that anybody would even consider it. "THAT book?" she asked, turning to glare at me. "Nigger, nigger, nigger."

I smiled, embarrassed. "I know," I nodded. "That's a hurdle. I don't know.... I think it'll be worth it." And in that instant, I was sure it would be. Call it a hunch or a simple "I'll show you" response to what she said, I was determined to teach *Huckleberry Finn*—warts and all.

When I walked back to the book room a little while later, I knew what

Introduction

I had to do. Walking in, it was as if the old guy himself was blowing a smoke ring in my direction. I kept staring at these books, envisioning these kids, these neglected kids, so hungry for a sign that someone acknowledges them and their existence. I could just see them nodding once were done reading it. "Yeah, they didn't want us reading it but hey, this Twain dude," they'd say. "He be straight."

Looking back in time, maybe it was my way of showing them—through Twain—that not only me, but a lot of other white people believed in fairness, in equality; that slavery, to me, was our country's original sin.

Maybe, later in the year, I'd get to a place with them where I could tell about how that sin still haunts some of us: my drive from Michigan to Florida about 25 years ago, noting the names of Civil War battlefields all along the way. I was just sailing along, a beautiful August morning, my music blaring when suddenly, I turned a corner and bang, I came upon an empty cotton field. I'd never seen one, never experienced one. It hit me. Slavery happened here. I began to choke up, tears welling in my eyes. It was an amazingly uncomfortable and surprising reaction. I pulled the car over. Where was this emotion coming from?

I was a long way from ever teaching. I'd come down here to be a writer. But now, years later, planning on teaching *Huck*, that moment flashed back to me, the power of it.

Could I, through Huck, help show these young black people that there were *some* white people who hated slavery? I'd seen some of that before in teaching Henry Thoreau and his principled anti-slavery stance, how it landed him in a Concord jail for a night. Once the kids learned about Henry, about his life, his quirks, the kids loved him. Called him their friend. And he was a lot less lovable than Huck.

The more I thought about it, somebody had to put those books into action and loose Twain's enchanting words on these kids. Why, it would be like freeing butterflies out of a cigar box. As I wheeled the book cart back to my classroom, the more I was sure I was right. Wouldn't Huck's hardscrabble life fit perfectly at my school? If Huck was alive, hell, wouldn't he *go* to my school? Wouldn't he fit in?

Here he was, a victim of child abuse, the son of a horribly racist town drunk, a kid who felt unwanted. Wouldn't Huck strike a sadly familiar chord with so many of these young people raised by a single mom or a grandma, a dad unknown or incarcerated, a long, sad trail of trouble stretching in every direction? These are hard truths; probably not the kind of thing you'd want to say about the kids you teach but it was—and is—reality.

More than that, wouldn't they find—didn't they need—a moral compass in their own lives to mirror the one in this extraordinary tale of two absolute misfits who cared about each other; one who was willing to go, as he so movingly says, "to Hell" to help the other? For young people who are growing up outside of and in some cases, generally uncared for by the system, wouldn't Huck's ability to survive, to live by his wits, give them something no other novel I could think of would? Hope?

Sure, there would be hurdles—there always are, attempting to connect with this over connected generation—but couldn't they be overcome? We would find out. We'd go at this strategically, carefully but also with a bit of the "we're getting away with something" enthusiasm that fired some of Twain's finest work.

The more I considered it, the more that seemed the right way to go. Let them feel like we're sliding this in under the wire, smuggling it into the classroom, this controversial book that some people didn't think they should read, but hey, you guys decide. That seemed like a good plan. I began to strategize. Before we began reading *Huck*, I'd explain to them how Twain wrote it.

For teachers trying to inspire and instruct high school students in the art of writing, Twain is, in many ways, the perfect guy to study. He is relentless, has an extraordinary vocabulary and a commanding presence on the page, a style of writing that, at its best, is almost hypnotic. And he's funny!

Think about the writers you had to study in school. How many of them made you laugh? Dickens can be funny, but for a high schooler, the humor is as crumbly as a stale crumpet. Shakespeare is witty and immensely clever, but his humor is deeper and sharper than most high schoolers can connect with. You generally don't hear many "ha-ha's" during *Romeo and Juliet* or *Macbeth*. Same goes for Nathaniel Hawthorne as well as his rather intense friend, that jokester Herman Melville. Don't forget quirky old Edgar Allen Poe. The kids did love the rich irony of naming a guy who is to be stonewalled alive "Fortunato" (in his classic "Cask of Amontillado.") You can hear Poe laughing bitterly to himself as he scrawls that name in black ink on the manuscript, can't you?

We're talking here, of course, about connection. Trying to find a way to connect with your students wherever you have to go. As we studied the

Introduction

early Twain readings (contained in the Appendix) building up to *Huck*, we got a sense of the man's style. Twain has an unerring ability to write you into scenes of laughter, of comedy, where the students, even the ones not paying particularly close attention, get the jokes and laugh. He sometimes writes as if he feels a censor or some schoolmarm looking over his shoulder tiptoes right up to the line of decency and correctness and proper behavior and sticks a toe or two or three over the line, just to see what he can get away with. Sometimes, that spirit is contagious. To everybody.

"Mr. Nogo," a student asked one afternoon, "can we use profanity in this?"

"Hell, no," I said. Why not have a little fun?

What also seemed to attract my students, who are, if you did not already know this, very definitely anti-outlining, anti-planning, anti-rough drafts, was that Twain worked with no map, no pre-writing plan. Judging from everything we've read about his writing methods, Mr. Clemens sat down, lit a cigar and went for it.

Now, he did, of course, go back and prune—*Huck*'s manuscript pages show that. But it doesn't read that way. So, for kids who usually have a problem getting started, kids who are afraid to be wrong, Twain shows them that there's no reason to be hesitant, to carry their idea as far as their inspiration can or should logically take them. Maybe even farther.

I remember an epic argument about that very point with my Rivier College professor, Sister Marjorie Francoeur, many years ago. In her American literature course, she taught novels in pairs and had matched Twain's *A Connecticut Yankee in King Arthur's Court* with a novel by Twain's friend and confidante, William Dean Howell. Howell's book was *The Rise of Silas Lapham*. On the afternoon of our presentation, knowing my Twain allegiance, she stood right in front of me, this 5-foot dynamo in a black and white habit, and tore into Twain, my hero, for his excesses and anachronisms and just plain wild moments in *Court*. These gaffes, she said, weakened the work. He tried to do too much, she said. It was a valid point.

But I fought back, bravely, given the circumstances: me, a high school jock trying to figure out college and the writers he loved, swimming in a sea of sophomore Catholic girls. Maybe it didn't matter to anyone else in that class what she said about Twain, about art, but it did to me. I had to stick up for Twain, for all those writers whose reach exceeds their grasp. Any time a writer writes, there's no reason *not* to go for it, to reach for the stars, as it were, instead of settling for a smaller, less ambitious, more perfectly crafted project. That was my writer's philosophy, and she helped me realize that.

To me, it was far less daring to do what Howells did, carefully writing a nifty, seamless tale about a crappy little paint factory that wasn't going to upend anybody's psyche. Nice story, but do you *have* to read it? No. Twain was tackling more important topics like war and manipulation and royalty and superstitions and prejudice? So what if there was excess? Let the writer have his say. Isn't *Hamlet* four hours long? Was James Joyce writing *Ulysses* worrying about the general reader? Who are the writers writing for, anyway, the critics? At this point in my life, I'd hardly written a word yet; I was barely toe-deep into my college career. Yet this discussion mattered to me, and Twain mattered to me. Now, all these years later, perhaps he could live again in my classroom. Maybe he would matter to my kids, too.

Let me admit that right here, with classical, college-approved and structured training as an educator, some might not have even considered teaching *Huck Finn* in a setting like mine. Too controversial, too old, too difficult for struggling readers. But I went on feeling, not Lexile levels or its readability index. It was a bit of a gamble.

I'd never imagined myself teaching—ever. Though now, I do remember my wonderful American history teacher, Mary Ann Civitello, once turning over her class to me to explain the importance of *The Federalist Papers* and Alexander Hamilton's far-reaching (and, to me, way more sensible than Thomas Jefferson's) theories about the future of this country. But that was a one-time thing. Upon graduation, I embarked on a career as a sportswriter, editor and columnist, writing for newspapers in New England, Michigan and Florida. Though continuing to read lots and lots of other writers, I always seemed to come back to Twain, who also began his career as a journalist. Who knew that someday I'd want to teach his works?

How did I start teaching? A few years into my newspaper career in Florida, I had a conversation one morning with Mike Gillespie, then the head basketball coach of Tallahassee Community College. We were talking about something I'd written and Gillespie looked up at me, in the middle of one of my sentences, and said, "You need to teach."

"Me? Are you serious?"

"Yeah," he said. "Anybody this serious, this passionate about writing,

Introduction

you ought to share that. I'm going to set it up." He did. I met with Dr. Sam Cunningham, then the communications department chair. He asked me what would I do if I taught freshman English? I explained my ideas, explaining the class should be practical, challenging, and useful. I wanted to use music and video. "It sure wouldn't be like my high school English classes," I remember saying, his eyes brightening. "I'd make it interesting."

And I wanted to use Twain. There's so much that he's written that's useful to a teacher. If you explain it and frame it, these high school kids would connect, too. Especially with *Huck*.

So, having had a few years of experience with this wonderful novel, *The Adventures of Huckleberry Finn* is a book that can get your students to connect in a way that few books can. Using a few of Twain's other works spread out through the year—just a smidgen of them included here—can help you take your classes somewhere unusual, some place you might not be able to get to with the standard English class fare. Let most of America continue to slam the standards of *The Great Gatsby* and *Pride and Prejudice* and *Night* and *The Scarlet Letter* down these kids' throats. There are many ways to teach and for some, maybe even most schools, these works will be fine.

That was not an option for me. The plan was to take my kids somewhere else, to see if they could really appreciate a writer who thought and wrote differently, someone who didn't mind putting America on notice when it took incredible courage to do so. While we will never exactly know what Twain had in mind with *Huck Finn*, it seems abundantly clear that the character of Jim is drawn with great affection and pride and, considering he made an unlettered slave the book's true hero in 1885, genuine courage.

And there was this: in an unfortunate era of continued racial strife, whether it's Ferguson or Dallas or Minnesota or who knows where else will have erupted by the time this book comes out, is it so wrong to offer up *Huck Finn*'s enduring message of friendship and loyalty to an entire generation that might not see much of that anywhere else?

It's certainly true that the book does seem to draw more than its share of controversy on an annual basis—you can almost write the headline and story and wait for some angry parent to holler at some school board; in 2017, it was Virginia and Maryland; Pennsylvania and Minnesota the year before that. *Huck* remains a novel that can be a joy to teach and one that will likely stick with your students, as it stuck with mine.

Why **Huck?** *Why Now?*

In *Teaching* Huckleberry Finn, I'm hoping to share some of the things that brought this remarkable novel to my students. In addition to my walk through *Huck*, I wanted to share the six separate Twain pieces we used to begin the semester. Some are famous, and some you've probably never heard of. These five pieces are culled for you in the Appendix. They are: "Running for President," "An Encounter With an Interviewer," "How I Edited an Agricultural Paper," "An Entertaining Article," "The Private Habits of Horace Greeley," and "Cooper's Literary Offenses." Using any of these as a prelude or supplement to the novel will give your classes a real sense of Twain, his unusual writing style and wit.

Once we finished reading *Huck*, we also used two superb supplemental pieces to help us look at the novel from a broader perspective. As anyone who's ever taught *Huck* knows, Twain's ending has always drawn a great deal of criticism from the critics and literary experts who've called it disappointing. This was worth examining.

To refresh your memory, as the book winds down, runaway slave Jim is in captivity at the Phelps' farm and Huck's mission is to free him. Lo and behold, who arrives just in time to help him but his old friend Tom Sawyer, supposedly visiting his aunt? This is where, for some, the book goes off the rails. Obviously, it's a real stretch to imagine Tom just happens to show up where Jim is being hidden. That's one thing. But when Tom arrives and takes over the plan to free Jim, and comes up with this long list of crazy Sir Walter Scott-ish things he insists Jim must do while in chains before he and Huck can break Jim free, Huck just sort of shrugs and goes along with it. To many, well, that doesn't seem like something Huck would do then. Here's Huck, who has seemed to grow in stature with almost every page, suddenly reverting back as the obedient Tom Sawyer follower we see at the beginning of the novel. To Ernest Hemingway and many other writers and critics, Twain kind of blew it here. That's been the conventional wisdom.

Brilliantly, writer Maria Konnikova considered the decades of Twain criticism on this point and weighed it against what we know about modern psychology and wasn't so sure that what Twain imagined Huck might do if Tom returned was that far off the mark. In a wonderful article written for *Scientific American* (also included in the Appendix), Konnikova spoke with psychologists about Huck's behavior and, remarkably, they backed Mr. Clemens' rendering of the Tom-Huck relationship in the book's much-maligned finish: "I won't argue for or against the ending's artistic merits,"

Introduction

she writes, "That's a topic for another piece. But what I will say is that psychologically, Huck's about-face couldn't be more sound. Twain might have offended on other accounts, but there is one thing he got right: not only could Huck fall back to old ways at the tip of a hat—or the arrival of a Tom Sawyer, as the case may be—but he most likely would do so if he were a flesh-and-blood twelve-year-old fresh off a rafting adventure."

Really? Well, now, Ms. Konnikova, tell us more: "As Leo Marx put it in a 1953 essay, when Tom enters the picture, Huck falls "almost completely under his sway once more, and we are asked to believe that the boy who felt pity for the rogues is now capable of making Jim's capture the occasion for a game. He becomes Tom's helpless accomplice, submissive and gullible." "And to Marx," she writes, "this regressive transformation is as unforgiveable as it is unbelievable. From a literary standpoint, perhaps it is unforgiveable; it is not for me, here, to judge. But psychologically, the reversion is as sound as it gets, despite the fury that it inspires." Now, this is heavy, first-rate literary theory, ripe for discussion and exactly the kind of close reading and critical thinking that your students will need and don't get. Konnikova's terrific article, in full, is available in the Appendix (thanks again, Maria!)

The other important addition to "Teaching" is the addition of author George Saunders' "The United States of Huck," an imaginative new introduction to *Huckleberry Finn*, which was in his 1997 book *The Braindead Megaphone* and written for a new edition of Modern Library Classics. A superb award-winning writer himself, Saunders brings a fresh approach to the classic novel in his "United States of Huck," seeing the Tom-Huck relationship as representative of our unique American spirit, our collective blood. A huge Twain fan, Saunders admits he struggled at first attempting to write about Huck. But once he gets going, he dives fathoms deep:

> The difference between Tom and Huck is that Huck believes in the reality of what he sees and feels, and Tom does not. Tom believes in what he has read in books, or, more correctly, in the concepts that have arisen from what he has read in books. Huck believes in the reality of the people and things he sees, whereas to Tom, these things are only imperfect imitations of the people and things about which he has read. Because Huck believes that other people are real, he also believes in the reality of their suffering; he grieves when he hurts Jim, worries about the drunken rider at the circus, feels bad for betraying Miss Watson, and, most importantly, understands how much Jim needs his freedom.
>
> To Tom, Jim is not real, nor is Jim's suffering; Jim's suffering is simply an opportunity for Tom's ego and cleverness to exert themselves. He prolongs and

Why Huck? *Why Now?*

worsens this suffering by putting Jim through an insane ritual of escape a la those in Walter Scott novels (the low-comic riff that was Twain's Apparent Narrative Rationale at that time) and by withholding from Jim the staggering truth: Jim has been free for most of the novel, because Miss Watson emancipated him on her deathbed.

This is some first-class insight into these characters, guaranteed to get your students discussing the work and, once they go a little further, maybe consider the very nature of their own country. Saunders sees the two of them as representative as two distinct strains of American thought:

> Huck and Tom represent two viable models of the American Character. They exist side by side in every American and American action. America is, and always has been, undecided about whether it will be the United States of Tom or the United States of Huck. The United States of Tom looks at misery and says: Hey, I didn't do it. It looks at inequity and says: All my life I have busted my butt to get where I am, so don't come crying to me. Tom likes kings, codified nobility, unquestioned privilege. Huck likes people, fair play, spreading the truck around. Whereas Tom knows, Huck wonders. Whereas Huck hopes, Tom presumes. Whereas Huck cares, Tom denies. These two parts of the American Psyche have been at war since the beginning of the nation, and come to think of it, these two parts of the World Psyche have been at war since the beginning of the world, and the hope of the nation and of the world is to embrace the Huck part and send the Tom part back up the river where it belongs.
> But this not what happens in Huck Finn…

More on this, deeper into the book.

As a teacher, you'll find these additional articles add depth and complexity to Twain's classic. By using all this material and perhaps some you might have already dug up, teachers can share this remarkable novel with future generations wrestling with the same kinds of moral boundaries Twain tackled over a hundred years earlier.

To me and my students, they reveal a writer who was fearless, willing to explore almost any idea. At my school, often dealing with non-readers, struggling students unaccustomed to academic success, kids often hesitant to expand their ideas or even have one when it came time to write, Twain encouraged them to go further. Similarly, *Teaching* Huckleberry Finn is intended as an encouragement, a spark to help English teachers everywhere—and maybe just plain readers—to enjoy, devour, savor the work of one of America's most significant writers.

While the focus is on *Huckleberry Finn,* Twain's greatest work, there are so many things in his writing that can be useful, informative, and exciting,

Introduction

even. I hope you'll find many of these things throughout these pages. Over the years in my classes at my school, the book has had an impact I couldn't have imagined. And while it isn't always easy—as my issues this year and last showed—it is worth it. *Huckleberry Finn* is always—and will always—be worth it.

1

Wrestling with the "N" Word

Before we read a single page of Twain's classic novel, I thought it was important to show them the writer's life as it was in 1880. Using a clip from the Ken Burns' Mark Twain documentary about his little summer gazebo at Quarry Farm, a spot secluded in the rolling hills of upstate New York, they saw that Twain would work all day, undisturbed, often straight through lunch. Then in the evenings, he'd bring those pages back to the house, gather the family and read that day's work with his wife, Livy, serving as the first set of ears and editor. He got immediate feedback. What feedback do these kids get in their daily lives? Why not let them imagine a real, connected family—something most of them didn't know. That would sort of model how we would do it in class. We'd read it together, then talk about it.

Looking ahead to the year with my class, I remembered reading Twain's daughter, Susy, recreating those summer evenings:

> Papa read Huckleberry Finn to us in manuscript just before it came out, and then he would leave parts of it with mamma to expurgate, while he went off up to the study to work, and sometimes Clara and I would be sitting with mamma while she was looking the manuscript over, and I remember so well, with what pangs of regret we used to see her turn down the leaves of the pages, which meant that some delightfully dreadful part must be scratched out. And I remember one part pertickularly which was perfectly fascinating it was dreadful, that Clara and I used to delight in, and oh with what dispair we saw mamma turn down the leaf on which it was written, we thought the book would be almost ruined without it. But we gradually came to feel as mamma did.

Hearing a kid have real input on her dad's work, yeah, that is something. Now it's hinted that Twain put some things in just so his wife would have something to take out, just to liven things up at the old homestead. Wasn't that what we were doing? It was clear that to Twain, the kids' reactions mattered. It would again. Had these kids ever talked about slavery? Or friendship? Or doing the right thing? This novel would get them talking about that, at the very least.

From my non-educational background, I saw the great goal of any teacher is to get kids engaged, to really know the man and his characters, especially Huck and Jim, their great ancestor. If I could do that ... why, that class could flow like the Mississippi herself...

Start with the "N" word. It's a must. Though early American authors like Frederick Douglass and Harriet Beecher Stowe and others before Twain did use the "n" word hundreds of times in their books without it ever becoming an issue, in 2017 or later, you simply have no choice but to begin your present discussion of the novel with that word. Ugly as it is. It is a time bomb.

In the summer of 2017, for example, comedian Bill Maher—who has made a career out of being about as liberal a political commentator as the law allows—got himself into a nasty little snit after making an off-hand remark, calling himself "a house nigger" (instead of being willing to work in a Nebraska cornfield, as jokingly invited by Nebraska Senator Ben Sasse). It was a joke, or intended to be one.

Maher has always been a supporter of civil rights and no commentator anywhere was quicker to question the then-Republican candidate Trump on what appeared to be his very questionable racial stances. No commentator anywhere seemed to be more passionate about fairness and civil rights.

But suddenly, the world was all over him. Even ex-rapper Ice Cube appeared on a subsequent show to lecture Maher on when he could use the word (never) and when he couldn't (ever). All over one word. A word you're hard pressed not to find on what seems like 70 percent of the rap music out there. Will it ever die?

Twain, of course, didn't know this in 1885. But it is amazing that the one word has, in some sad cases, sent allegedly educated, professional people running from the book.

So ... first up, you need to deal with the "N" word. How far you want to go with it is up to you. Gathering resources for the book, one valuable program that I wanted to use was the "Great Books" series' episode on *Huck Finn* (available on YouTube). But listening to educator John Wallace criticize the book (calling it "the most grotesque racist trash ever written") makes me think a) he hasn't read the entire book and b) he doesn't get out

1. Wrestling with the "N" Word

much. Wallace certainly seems to be the go-to guy when you want somebody to take a stand against the book. His impassioned criticism against the book is featured prominently in many places. Depending on your situation, this debate can really open your discussion of the book and the "N" word.

As for me, teaching in a school whose enrollment was 99 percent African-American, I chose to skip that part of the video, at least to start with. For one thing, we already hear that word several times a day in our hallways and lunchrooms, though I wish we didn't. Showing the kids an agitated African-American educator speaking passionately against a book we hadn't read yet just might tilt them away before they gave *Huck* a fair chance.

Another thing I've learned about teaching racial issues at our school: if you open that door, you never know what you'll get in response or how quickly. Writing this in the summer of 2017, the rather unbelievable response to the Kendall Jenner Pepsi ad has finally quieted down. In case you missed it, this well-intended soft drink commercial opens with a city in the middle of some sort of protest, something that's not really defined, but a protest formidable enough to have what seems like hundreds of millennials on the march. Swept up in the moment, the impressionable Jenner walks away from what seems like a posh modeling job, sheds her makeup (a major concession!) and joins the protest march, which finally comes to a halt when they run into a string of young policemen. The music swells, Jenner walks up to one young officer, offers him a Pepsi and everyone cheers. Everyone, that is, but those who saw the commercial as diminishing the Black Lives Matter movement.

When I showed it to my students, all of whom were black (but one), they had no measurable response—so what, they said. Then they went home, talked amongst themselves and evidently went online. The next day, facing a writing assignment, suddenly many of them "were too outraged to even write about it." I dropped the assignment.

With Hip-Hop and rap perpetuating the use of the "N" word in black culture, the word remains an every-day part of their world. Hearing it uttered many days in my classroom—not okay under normal circumstances—was going to be strange. But while we were doing Huck, the word was essential to understanding Twain's intent for the book.

Twain wanted authenticity. That was, in his mind, the most effective way to get it: to write in Huck's voice as someone living in the 1840's would

Teaching *Huckleberry Finn*

have written it. At the same time, as an older white man, hearing the word "nigger" come out of my mouth somewhat regularly could be really disconcerting for some students (and for a couple, it was). One wise teacher, wiser than me, said when she read aloud from the novel, she would just skip over that word. Does that change the way students will read it? Or should read it? Good question. How did they feel about that word?

I began by asking my classes about their use of the word. Did they use it? Did their parents use it? What did they think of rappers using it all the time? Their answers were interesting and perhaps more layered than you might have expected. Many of them said that they used it but, "affectionately." How can one use *that* word affectionately? They continued. For some, it was a matter of spelling. "If I spell it 'niggaz,' that's not a bad word," explained one student. "Or nigga. It ain't the same word." Another student said, "It's like, 'Aw, Mr. Nogo, he's my nigga. It's a sign of affection, like, we tight."

After a little further discussion and some coaxing, more than a few admitted they used it in its regular, quite ugly, connotation and agreed they'd heard it all the time. But while it was—and is—ugly to me, it was not to them. "Only ugly to us when you say it," one student said.

Once you've had that discussion—and not before—you can begin to tackle the novel. Some teachers have, on occasion, even sent notes home, asking for permission. This is your call. I didn't do that, fearing it would give them an out that I feared they would almost surely take.

So ... after the discussion of the "N" word and its use in today's world, I began with a brief video clip that captures the most shocking and ugly moment in the novel they are about to read. A stunning clip from Hal Holbrook's fantastic one-man show *Mark Twain Tonight* blew them away (the *Huck Finn* excerpt is available on YouTube).

As you probably know, Holbrook has been doing the Twain one-man show for 50 years or more. If you've never seen it, he dresses as a 70-year-old Twain and talks to the audience about life, his career and in one memorable section, condenses his greatest work into a nine-minute condensation of the first half of *Huckleberry Finn*.

Using a young boy's voice, he begins with Twain's classic opening line—"You don't know about me without you have read a book..." then swiftly moves into Huck's meeting, later in the book, with a drunken Pap, which quickly becomes frightening.

Pap may be the single most reprehensible character in fiction, cer-

1. Wrestling with the "N" Word

tainly the worst in Twain. And here, Twain mirroring the racial sentiments of perhaps much of the American South at the time of this novel, shows Pap at his absolute worst. It is Election Day, and Pap is considering whether to go and vote. Then he happens upon a free black man, dressed in "the whitest suit you ever did see and the shiniest hat." And, to Pap's horror, he learns the man could vote. "Well, that let me out," he snarls, Holbrook perfectly capturing the hatred in Pap's (and, Twain implies, much of the American South's) heart. "Thinks I, what is the country a-comin' to?"

Here, teachers, is your chance to make a major point. At that time (1885) this may very well have been what many people south of the Mason/Dixon Line thought of black people. Maybe they wouldn't say it as hatefully as Pap does, but it's probably safe to say that was how they felt. By introducing this vicious racism to us readers this early, we get a true sense of the environment Huck grew up in. Perhaps we get a deeper understanding of the necessity of an author using such a word, to make that ugly world become real. That was my purpose for opening with that clip, too. After you've seen and heard that, there's nothing else in *Huck Finn* that would offend.

Because it is so cruel and upsetting, I showed my students—immediately after, usually the very same day—four outtakes from Ken Burns' *Mark Twain* DVD. If they think Twain used that word gratuitously, which I hope they do not, let's get these four Twain experts—including Holbrook and two African-American educators—to explain why they think Twain chose to use that awful word so often. If you have the DVD, it's on disc two in the special features. If you don't have it, it's well worth getting.

These four experts, authors Shelly Fisher Fishkin, African-American author David Bradley and African-American educator Jocelyn Chadwick and Holbrook discuss the use of the word and Twain's intent. Their words are eloquent and lay the groundwork for us to launch into the novel. Once the students watched those clips, we talked about what we saw and heard.

Before we opened the book, I tried to make sure to watch their faces, to see if any of them are upset or uncomfortable. Particularly since I teach in an African-American school, I tried to be sensitive, particularly as an older, occasionally cranky white guy. The opening of *Huck* is always a heavy day. That's why, when we actually begin the novel the next day and they hear Huck's free-flowing narrative voice combined with Twain's humor, well, it's uplifting. Unlike almost every other school text, it's *fun*.

Teaching *Huckleberry Finn*

As students settled in, before we turned to page one, we talked again about the controversy surrounding the book and how, in Twain's time, using the "N" word was no controversy at all. Since they are going to be hearing the word in our classroom, we need to be ready for it and right here, I usually give them a little historical perspective.

Andrew Levy's fine and valuable new book, *Huck Finn's America*, explains that the use of "nigger" wasn't at all controversial when the book came out in February of 1885. Why, it wasn't even *mentioned* in the mostly favorable reviews at the time. Somewhat surprisingly, *Huckleberry Finn* wasn't even really seen by these reviewers as a book primarily about black/white relations. That may be the way it's been taught in America's schools for decades, but that's not how America saw it in 1885.

While *Huck* was banned by a library in Henry Thoreau's Concord in March for the novel's "low grade of morality" and "bad grammar," nobody mentioned the 200-plus uses of the word "nigger." Critics at the time were much more concerned about the impression the pipe-smoking, school-skipping Huck might leave on an impressionable youthful audience. As Levy explains early in his book, "Contemporary reviews of Twain's novel, dozens of which appeared in American newspapers in the spring of 1885, barely mentioned race at all; they talked about children and what message the book sent them, with great and varied passion."

Reading this, all these years later, is somewhat surprising. Have our vocabulary standards changed that much since 1885? If you take a few moments to read the reviews of the book, the "N" word was not mentioned by anyone. When the Concord Public Library banned the book, calling it "the veriest trash," the neighboring Massachusetts paper, the Springfield Republican, applauded their decision: "The Concord public library deserves well of the public by their action in banishing Mark Twain's new book, *Huckleberry Finn* on the grounds that it is trashy and vicious," they wrote, concluding that "(Twain's) literary skill is, of course, superior; but (their) moral level is low, and their perusal cannot be anything less than harmful." Moral level low? The whole point of *Huck* is morality! Reviewers...

In "The United States of Huck," George Saunders' terrific introduction to the 2001 edition of *Huckleberry Finn*, Saunders agrees that America's biggest concern at the time was that students, having read the book, might skip school, take to smoking corn cob pipes, and sleeping in hogsheads. Seems almost funny now.

1. Wrestling with the "N" Word

So as we begin to read and students hear the word "nigger" read aloud in their classroom, we talk about how somewhere between 1885 and now, it's as if the "N" word in *Huckleberry Finn* has become hot, bold type, yelling at you off its pages.

[Note: I sometimes use an audiobook recording, letting the class hear Huck in another voice.]

As we began to read, you could see the students wince when the "N" word came up, particularly in the first two chapters. The first heavy usage comes in chapter two. Be ready. I usually try to do both chapters the same day. By using an audiobook, it's easy to pause it once you first hear that word—and measure their responses. There are hundreds of versions available, some on YouTube as well. It's also nice to have a professional reader give Huck a voice that'll ring in the kids' heads instead of yours.

In the charming and celebrated chapter one, we meet Huck, hear his voice, get a sense of him, and near the end of the chapter, he mentions the "N" word for the first time: "By and by, they fetched the niggers in and had prayers and everybody was off to bed." Scanning the classroom, there were a few mild looks, but that was about it. But in chapter two, things in the classroom can—and usually do—change quickly.

What happens is Tom Sawyer and Huck steal out into the night. They run into a sleeping Jim and Tom gets the idea for a prank. He takes the hat off Jim's head and hangs it on a branch directly above his head. When he awakens, Jim can only conclude that it was done by witches. And then comes the profusion of "N" words.

You hear things like Huck saying "niggers is always talking about witches in the dark by the kitchen fire," and "Niggers would come miles to hear Jim tell about it…" You could see the students looking at each other, the word, which seemed to echo around the classroom, made them uncomfortable. Some looked challengingly at me, as we listened. Sometimes, I read it out loud. Sometimes, they laughed out loud, like they were getting away with something.

Here was a good place to discuss what Twain was doing, my chance to encourage the students to trust the author, to go a little further into his work, to ask why Twain took such a risk. Or maybe it wasn't such a risk in 1885. As noted earlier, none of the reviewers even mentioned his use of the "N" word.

One student suggested that Huck's comment like this might very well be what a teenager in 1840 would have said, a great insight. It was important for them to understand that in 1840, using the "N" word wasn't denigrating, it was describing (or so non-black people told themselves.) There was a difference.

By the second day, the students seemed to be starting to understand. There were a few snickers here and there; you'll always have that. But in one class, the "N" word may have even had an effect I didn't anticipate. "I had no problem with the 'n' word," explained Jeremy, the football team's quarterback. "I guess because this is a new generation, it really didn't bother me as much. It really made the story more interesting by using the 'n' word."

As we continued through the novel, the shock of hearing the "N" word seemed to be diminishing. There are so many other things going on in *Huck* that after a while, it just seemed to slide by. Examined in a classroom setting, *Huck Finn* is one of those novels that you could sort of see or feel the book taking shape. You sense Twain figuring out his characters and his novel as he continued, a writer figuring it out and making it up as he went.

When your students notice this, take the opportunity to discuss Twain's authorial methods, which were driven wholly by inspiration and not by outline or following a carefully wrought plan. As William Dean Howells said, as quoted in Saunders' "The United States of Huck," "Mr. Clemens is the first writer to use in extended writing the fashion we all use in thinking, and to set down the thing that comes into his mind without fear or favor of the thing that went before or the thing that may be about to follow.... He would take whatever offered itself to his hand out of that mystical chaos, that divine ragbag, which we call the mind, and leave the reader to look after relevancies and sequences for himself."

This may also explain why Twain ran out of enthusiasm for the manuscript at several points, putting the book down for years at a time until he figured out where to take it next. Since, in my experience, one of the most puzzling things for my teen writers to do was elaborate, carry the story, the sentences onward, you can use Twain as an example. What did he do? How did he make the novel move? What should happen next? I'd often close out that day's lesson by asking the class that question. Just to plant that thought in their head. Would they read ahead to see if they were right? Not a bad idea, is it, Mr. Nogo?

For many high school students, elaboration is an issue. It's tough enough for some of them to get one sentence down. Now you're telling me to write *another*?

1. Wrestling with the "N" Word

One somewhat odd method I used to demonstrate elaboration and one method of expanding their thoughts was playing a Monty Python skit about a killer joke, a man who creates a joke that is deadly. The clip opens with a man writing the joke, reading it to himself and dying, of laughter, literally. So, you've got a joke that is deadly. Now what?

In comes his wife, she reads it, laughs herself to death. Next, let's bring in Scotland Yard, how will they extract the deadly joke with no further loss of life? Oops, there goes an Inspector. We even wrote a diagram on the board of how the comedy group carried their ideas through ... from Scotland Yard—under incredible precautions—to the British army who decided to use the joke as a weapon in World War II, translating the joke into German, and so on. The point is, they ended up a long way from where they started, which is what elaboration and expanding your thinking is all about.

As you read *Huck Finn* with young readers, it's a great novel to show them that your imagination can take you amazing places. Look what Twain did. You never get the sense—at least, I don't—that Twain had this whole plot written out somewhere. He thought of it as he went, trusting his brain and imagination to make the connections. And by trusting the muse, often enough, it did.

One story I always share with my students is about an assignment from my days teaching at a community college. I was trying to teach my students how to compare and contrast and the assignment asked them to write a description of their bedroom at age 10 and their bedroom now, wherever they were.

My intent, of course, was to contrast the various ages, adulthood gradually creeping into their lives, how they would capture and maybe interpret the differences. The one I remember best was by a student who wrote this lovely, picture-perfect description of her room back in Oklahoma, almost as if she had a photographic memory. Then, as she began to describe her room near the college, a muted but unmistakable sadness took over the story. She carefully described the messy room, the books on the bed, the photos from home distributed around the room— it was so well done, the class was utterly silent; she had commanded the page.

Then, when she got to the final sentence and the heavy final sentence... "And over on the wall, (pause) I can see my calendar (pause) with the number of days marked off *until I get to go home.*"

Teaching *Huckleberry Finn*

That's how the piece ended and there wasn't a dry eye anywhere, including me. Those details, mounting one on top of another until the effect was devastating, did it. When I complimented her on the surprising power of her piece, she protested, "But, Mr. Nogo, I didn't even know what I was doing." To me, that was the beauty of it. She trusted her muse.

2

A Rich Tapestry of Themes

One of the genuinely exciting aspects of getting to teach a novel like *Huckleberry Finn* is Twain's writing is so rich and full of rumblings that he has the knack of being able to raise so many themes and ideas, seemingly off-hand. Having read the novel and taught it many times, it seems as if there's always another idea or theme that emerges the next time through.

A former teacher friend of mine noted this as well and, in a note to me, suggested that one thing that might be helpful to other teachers or professors is the time allotment. How much time do you take with *Huckleberry Finn*? I'd say for me, it was generally close to a month, but that depended on the progress of the class, how they were responding to the work and how deep they wanted to go. With some classes, at least in my experience, they were so into the book, they loved reading the critics' comments and discussing it after we'd finished reading it. So, my answer might seem a cop-out, but really, it's how deep do you want to go?

The themes begin to pop up right away in chapter three. After the Tom and Huck hijinks of chapter two, Twain effortlessly stumbles into one of the more fascinating themes of the book, religion. One of the great discoveries for Twain had to be what he could do with Huck, as he called him "an unwashed boy" as his mouthpiece. When you sit back and look at how easily Twain makes it happen, it's marvelous. A religious skeptic himself, he always had a lot of questions about religion. With Huck wrestling with these major moral issues, it's a perfect vehicle for further discussion.

After his evening excursion with Tom Sawyer in the opening chapter, the next morning, Huck gets a well-earned scolding, saying Miss Watson "took me in the closet and prayed, but nothing come of it" (ha!—you can imagine Twain's eyebrow rising. Hmmm). Huck says, "She told me to pray every day and whatever I asked for I would get it. But it warn't so. I tried it. Once I got a fish-line, but no hooks. It warn't any good to me without hooks. I tried for the hooks three or four times, but somehow, I couldn't make it work. By and by, one day, I asked Miss Watson to try for me, but she said I was a fool. She never told me why, and I couldn't make it out no way."

A kid wonders about praying. Is God really listening? What can you pray for? A new car? A boyfriend? A good grade? Though my students, almost to a one, would describe themselves as religious, this idea hadn't really hit them, it seemed. As a teacher, if you read their eyes, get a feel for where they really *are* as they're taking this all in, you know the moments to pause and discuss. This was one of the first ones.

"What *can* you pray for?" I asked them, looking them all directly in the eye from one side of the class to another. A hand goes up in the back of the room. "Lunch." Ok, so we'd have to work on this.

As the chapter continues, Twain sends Huck off into the woods where he sits down to think about it. And he asks some very good questions: "If a body can get anything they pray for," Huck wonders, "why don't Deacon Winn get back the money he lost on pork? Why can't the widow get back her silver snuff box that was stole? Why can't Miss Watson fat up?"

The students were laughing—Twain's intent, of course. But the questions are good ones, aren't they? What does God listen to? Sure, God is great, He provides. And yet so many of these students of mine seemed to have been dealt what seemed to many a pretty lousy hand. No dad, and mom not real reliable. No money. But many of them had faith. Or at least, they said they did. But Huck, I think, was struggling with that concept. That interested them.

"Sometimes," Huck says, "the widow would take me one side and talk to me about Providence in a way to make a body's mouth water; but maybe next day, Miss Watson would take hold and knock it all down again. I judged I could see there was two Providences, and a poor chap would stand considerable show with the widow's Providence, but if Miss Watson's got him, there warn't no help for him anymore."

They were quiet. "Is Heaven a reward?" I asked them. "How good do you have to be to go to Heaven? Do you think God is watching you all the time?" There were looks all around. This is heavy stuff and we're in chapter three. I looked directly at the kid who made the lunch comment earlier and smiled: "You better hope not."

2. A Rich Tapestry of Themes

As chapter three continues, Tom convinces Huck and his "gang" that they need to be robbers. It's all Tom Sawyer kind of stuff, Huck's practicality questioning all this talk about A-rabs and "julery" to the point that when you get to the end of the chapter, there seems a clear divide between the two, at last. Tom, caught up in his imagination and his half-interpreted classics, will be happy to keep manipulating the innocents. Not Huck. Not anymore.

"So then I judged all that stuff was only one of Tom Sawyer's lies" [Note: remember, *lies* in those days, was a *huge* insult]. "I reckoned he believed in the A-rabs and the elephants, but as for me I think different. It had all the marks of a Sunday School." With that stunning sentence, most critics see Huck leaving Tom in the dust. As the esteemed critic Leo Marx wrote back in 1953: "The fact is that Huck has rejected Tom's romanticizing of experience; moreover, he has rejected it as part of the larger pattern of society's make-believe, typified by Sunday school."

In other words, he's growing up. Which, of course, foreshadows all that Huck is about to go through in the subsequent chapters, including faking his own death, watching all his friends mourn him and other fun things. Again, look at the themes you could discuss. What would it be like to witness your own funeral? Who are your truest friends? Who really seemed to mourn you? What friends didn't show up?

Twain has remarked that he began *Huck Finn* as a sequel to Tom Sawyer. Through the first three chapters, that's easy enough to believe. There's no sense of a dramatic trip down the Mississippi or any life-threatening event. It seems as if it'll be more like Tom Sawyer, just written in the first person. But by chapter four, when Huck sees Pap's heel print in the snow (a cross—interesting symbol, no?) we know things have changed dramatically.

First, Huck says he's going to get rid of his inheritance he won at the end of Tom Sawyer (or else Pap will want it for whiskey) and second, he starts thinking about his future, which we conclude, means he needs to skedaddle. Another theme; could your students give away their inheritance? Why doesn't Huck seem to care about money? For those days, he had a lot of it, yet never uses it. Hmmm.

Once he learns of Pap's return, he consults Jim and his hairball (theme: superstitions?) and then, in chapter five, Pap arrives looking for Huck's money and after an ugly scene, in chapter six, Pap kidnaps his own son and holes him up in a cabin where Huck decides after a few beatings and one frightening delirium tremens episode with his drunken father—the students were particularly attentive throughout this segment—decides he has to leave (theme: child abuse—what choices do children have?).

Huck's brilliance here, faking his own death in a most convincing and inspired way, wowed the kids. Just as, in the middle of the chapter, they were again reminded of Pap's villainy, hearing once again the ugly speech that we listened to as we opened the novel.

By the time you get to chapter six, Pap's ugly (and thankfully, only) soliloquy on race relations, voting privileges and other things, the students should be better prepared for a replay of the scene they saw acted out by Holbrook in *Mark Twain Tonight* on the first day of Huck.

Generally, I don't mention that we've read/watched this scene before. Let them make the discovery themselves. What happens is Pap has gone to town, learned that his court case (to get Huck, and more important to Pap, Huck's money) isn't going well. Not only that, he happened upon a well-dressed, free black man on the road. And he tells Huck exactly what he thinks about it.

The writing is brilliantly, scathingly ugly; baring the soul of a real racist is a revolting thing and as Pap carries on, you can see his hate so clearly—and sadly, this does not seem unfamiliar to my class. That is, they do not seem to be surprised to hear it. "He's so awful," one student said. "Idiot," added another. "Scum," blurted a third. "Exactly Twain's point," I said. "And notice how Twain takes some of the sting out of it." "How?" they asked. "As he so often does, with humor," I explained. We went back and noticed that as Pap is haranguing on, Twain describes that he has a couple of toes leaking out of one of his boots. Which, after he absently takes a comical tumble over a tub of salt pork, decides to fetch the tub a mighty kick with—you guessed it—the leaky boot.

There was a rumble of laughter and students noted how even at its ugliest moment (I doubt there are any who dispute that this moment is it) *Huck Finn* has a leavening, lightening humor, an ointment to take some of the sting away. If some of my students have been abused at home (their responses are sometimes revealing) they aren't at all surprised at Huck's next plan—the escape.

Once my students got a load of Huck's brilliantly faked death in chapter seven, some of them immediately found themselves relating to his thinking-on-his-feet intelligence (theme: is testing truly a measure of your intelligence?). They could tell that Huck was not the kind of kid who would

2. A Rich Tapestry of Themes

test well, but put him in a James Bond–like situation and watch him go. What I found fascinating was to read a line or two, and then have the kids explain what they thought Huck was doing and why he was doing it. Though only a teenager, Huck seems to be able to figure things out: he's a survivor. Again, there seemed to be a connection with my students. Nothing is handed to him and it's okay. He figures it out.

And some of Huck's thoughts are intriguing. As you move on through the chapters, you'll find, as I mentioned earlier, that the novel is a treasure trove of topics for discussion, like religion. Earlier, Twain, a noted skeptic, finds creative methods to discuss the issue. By seeding the novel with these moments, Twain sets things up perfectly for a teachable moment in chapter eight where Huck, having faked his death, sees loaves of bread (Biblical image?) floating on the water, intending to lead the searchers to Huck's corpse. Huck busts out with, "And then something struck me. I says, now, I reckon the widow or the parson or somebody prayed that this bread would find me, and here it has gone and done it. So there ain't no doubt but there is something in that thing. That is, there's something in it when a body like the widow or the parson prays, but it don't work for me..."

This often leads to a frequently wonderful class discussion on prayer and Heaven. What will it be like? This usually prompts some lively answers and often some sarcasm. Instead of asking them to speak out loud, I asked them to write it down. "My idea of heaven?" one student penned, "This class to be over. Forever." In my classroom, the students were getting more comfortable talking about God and religion and that was interesting to me. And you can feel the power of the novel beginning to truly sink in.

While every class is different, as teachers well know, when dealing with *Huck Finn* over several years at my school, it seems by the end of the first week, the characters are starting to connect with them. And the "N" word is not as much of a distraction. Critics are not as tolerant, it seems. Most can't seem to get through the novel without writing about it, debating it, even, as recently as a few years ago, issuing a version of the novel *without it,* substituting the word "slave." My students were not in favor of that, but we'll discuss that later. As humorist and Twainophile Roy Blount, Jr., has written, the novel "will not behave. It will not lay down."

This has given some contemporary novelists like Jane Smiley a chance to go on the attack. When you see the power this novel is exerting over your classes, you can't help but think of how removed from this experience are some academics and authors like Smiley, whose criticism of the book seems unfair: "Surely the discomfort of many readers, black and white, and the censorship battles that have dogged Huck Finn in the last twenty years are understandable," she wrote in her 1996 Harper's article, "Say It Ain't So, Huck." "No matter how often the critics 'place in context' Huck's use of the word 'nigger,' they can never excuse or fully hide the deeper racism of the novel—the way Twain and Huck use Jim because they really don't care enough about his desire for freedom to let that desire change their plans. And to give credit to Huck suggests that the only racial insight Americans of the nineteenth or twentieth century are capable of is a recognition of the obvious–that blacks, slave and free, are human."

Of course, it'd be wonderful if 2017 values could be placed on an 1885 novel. Sadly, this narrow viewpoint minimizes both Twain and Huck's achievement in the pages of *Huck Finn*. It may—and evidently does—seem that for Smiley, acknowledging African Americans were human was not a big deal. Yet, if you think about it, for an uneducated teenager, a "nascent racist" as George Saunders calls him, who likely came from a long line of racists, folks who were not the least bit squeamish about slavery and punishing those who attempted to circumvent it, for that person to be able to rise above what he's been taught—which Huck clearly does—that *is* something important. Through the goodness of his heart, he finds a way to truly care about Jim, to *unlearn* what he's been taught from Pap to pulpit.

If Smiley had ever taught in a high school like mine—which I doubt—she'd see that she sold Twain (and Huck) short. I well remember a moment from my first year in teaching Huck. I was about to sit down for my lunch break when there was a knock at my door and a young black man, maybe 16, who was someone I'd see in about an hour, was standing on the other side. He had an eager look on his face, angst in his eye. When we began the project, he told me that he'd never read a whole book before. Though not the most focused student, something about Huck connected with him. "How can I help you?" I asked. "Mr. Nogo.... Is Jim going to get to Cairo today?" He really, *really* wanted to know. Now, he was going to see me in about an hour. He was missing his lunch by stopping by to ask me. I will not let myself forget the look in his eye, how it really *meant* something to him. And that this was no small thing. "I guess we'll have to see," I smiled at him. "How about if you start the reading today?"

Chapter eight also brings us the first face-to-face meeting of Huck

2. A Rich Tapestry of Themes

and Jim on Jackson's Island. Outcasts, escapees from the world they each seemed to be sentenced to, they know each other—Huck recognizes Jim right away. But they aren't friends, not yet. And wouldn't the novel be changed if they *were* friends beforehand? "Jim, ol' buddy, what are you doing here?" Instead, when he learns Jim had run off, it's "Jim!" meaning that Huck immediately understands he's talking to a runaway slave and that they both can be in hanging by his heels trouble.

Twain's genius here was to put two acquaintances together, two people who did have some things in common, who weren't particularly favored in their own community, who did think they knew each other but found out there was so much more there. This may be more philosophical than Twain intended, but isn't that true about people you think you know, but really don't?

Carefully, through the slips and falls and missteps of their time together, we see the birth of a miraculous friendship, one that in 1885 really seemed possible when in fact, it probably was not. This grouchy old cigar-smoking wise guy was showing us that as a nation, we could all get along together, that racial harmony, and just plain harmony, was possible.

He also unveiled one of his great skills: dialect. For the young reader, it also brings an obstacle. Using one of the seven (count 'em) dialects Twain takes immense pride in, Jim recounts his story to Huck, explaining his presence on the island, what he went through to get there and from these early stirrings, we see Jim trust Huck with what could be very incriminating details of his escape. Interesting in these days that they seem to be speaking two different languages.

As the chapter deepens, we begin to see where Twain is going with this. We see Huck admonish himself for listening to Jim's story, implicating himself but vowing to not relent: "I said I wouldn't and I'll stick to it," Huck tells Jim. "Honest *injun* I will. People would call me a low down Abolitionist and despise me for keeping mum—but that don't make no difference. I ain't agoing to tell, and I ain't agoing back there anyways."

In chapter ten, Twain brilliantly gives us a prank gone wrong, contrasting the difference between a kid and a grownup, how for one of them, this escape to Jackson's Island was more of a lark; for the other, he was literally running for his life. Though Huck has shown himself to be much more mature, here he reverts to a Tom Sawyer–like tactic. Huck kills a rattlesnake, puts it on Jim's blanket "thinking there'd be some fun" when Jim finds it. When the snake's mate curls itself around the body and bites

Teaching *Huckleberry Finn*

Jim on the heel, a bite that could be fatal, we get the first inkling that this escape can turn deadly for either one in a second. It's an illustration to Huck—and us—that this is not child's play or a children's story any more.

At this point, the reader can see that something is going to happen. Both runaways can't stay on Jackson Island forever. That wouldn't be much of a story. We figure they're going somewhere. What gives the story its tension is, as we learn in chapter eleven, they are being hunted. This idea is settling in with Huck who, feeling bored, decides he'll slip ashore and see what the word is. His reconnaissance mission—posing as Sarah Williams—also signals a shift in the story, if subtle. After a hilarious attempt to pose as a girl, Huck/Sarah learns from the chatty Mrs. Judith Loftus that people on the other side of the river have seen the smoke from their campfire and they all understand there's a $300 reward for catching the runaway slave. Interesting to note Twain's subtle point here about Pap, too. The reward for Pap is $200.

Huck, well, he's added several aliases by now, and can't wait to get back to Jim. As he does, notice, as Twain surely wants us to, how Huck breaks the news: "Git up and hump yourself, Jim! There ain't a minute to lose. They're after us." Not you, *us*. Though it will be a while till Huck definitively takes a stand on this issue, he's on board, and literally as they find a raft and head down the Mississippi.

Now that the two of them have left society behind for a world on the water, Twain gives us a sense of their developing friendship and Huck's maturation before our eyes. After a scary adventure on a wrecked ship ironically called the Walter Scott (named for an author whose work Twain despised) in chapters twelve and thirteen, we get a bit of standup comedy, a piece that Twain enthusiastically performed on his "Twins of Genius" book tour after the publication of *Huck*.

Chapters fourteen and fifteen, on the surface, offer a comical argument between Huck and Jim over King Solomon and the French language, but if you take a closer look, it's really an examination of two different mind sets; one, half-educated, that buys the myths that are handed down about the Bible and the world and another, uneducated perhaps, that views those stories and the ways of the universe with a more skeptical eye. It's not hard to imagine who Twain sided with.

If a great novel really unveils the soul of a character and lets us feel we know him, *Huckleberry Finn* is fully in our hearts now. As you read these two chapters—one funny, one serious—your mind takes you to

2. A Rich Tapestry of Themes

dozens of other arguments/discussions between the two as they drift down the Mississippi. There may be other books where we can imagine what *isn't* written as well as what is, but that is one part of Twain's genius here, all done expertly through Huck's voice. We see that it is not just an adventure story, but also a lesson in life, race relations, teenagers vs. grownups, etc. If one can use the phrase "deepens" in literary terms (never seen it), to me, *Huck Finn* deepens right here. First with humor, then with morality.

I always found this the perfect place to let the students try their hand at dialect, selecting two to come before the class and perform this scene. To pass the time on the raft, Huck decides to do a little reading to Jim. It is implied that Jim can't read, so he is very interested in what Huck tells him. And Huck, feeling his oats, talks down to Jim as a white teenager in 1840 might have to any black person who dared to question him. But at the same time, Huck recognizes that Jim makes a good debater, asking questions that Huck has not anticipated and can't really answer. In a way, it's a bit of comeuppance for Huck, a subtle point that leads directly into the confrontation in chapter fifteen that, considering the time and circumstances, was perhaps Twain at his most heroic.

For just as chapter fourteen leaves you laughing at Huck's frustration at his inability to convince Jim of his flawed thinking: "you can't learn a nigger to argue." A fierce, unrelenting fog envelops the two of them; Jim on the raft, Huck in a canoe and for the first time in the novel, they are separated.

The two continue down the river, and Twain's rich descriptions, particularly of the sounds carrying across the water in the fog and storm, carries the reader right along with them. When finally, and miraculously, Huck comes upon the raft, he finds Jim as Tom Sawyer did in chapter two, sleeping. And like Tom, Huck is spurred to pull a prank on Jim, and a monstrous mean one as it turns out. While it might be exactly the kind of thing a teenager would pull on an adult, particularly a vulnerable one, coming as it does after the argument in the preceding chapter, you truly get a sense that Huck wanted to make a fool of Jim, to take him down a peg before the white man. Though Twain doesn't come right out and say so, a close read—I recommend that—for this chapter particularly, goes further into Huck's psyche.

When he climbs up on the raft, instead of celebrating his reunion with Jim, he decides to pretend that he was on the raft with Jim the entire time. Jim awakens, sees Huck and is overjoyed, so much so that Huck is uncomfortable (whether he's uncomfortable that Jim is black and cares for him or that he has a genuine adult male worried about him is a wonderful essay question). Huck asks Jim if he's been drinking, wondering why he's talking so wild: "How does I talk wild?" Jim wonders. "How?" Huck responds. "Why, hain't you been talking about my coming back, and all that stuff as if I'd been gone away."

Jim can't believe it. He asks Huck a series of questions and Huck shrugs them off, telling Jim he must have *dreamed* all this. Generously, very generously, Jim backs off a bit, saying, "Well, den, I reck'n I did dream it, Huck; but dog my cats ef it ain't de powerfullest dream I ever see." Jim is being the gentleman here, trusting Huck or maybe tolerating his prank as a father might. And perhaps that would have been that. But that isn't enough for Huck.

Brilliantly, Twain has his white teenager try and rub the black man's face in Huck's prank. After Jim offers up a somewhat mystical interpretation of the "dream," and just as they are about to move past this potentially ugly episode, Huck sticks the knife in: "Oh, well, that's interpreted well enough, as far as it goes, Jim, but what does *these* things stand for?" Huck means the leaves, branches and other rubbish that the raft collected going through the hellacious storm. Huck is saying, "You dreamed it, stupid? Then how did this stuff get here? Explain that one."

Keep in mind, this is a teenager saying this to a grown man. A man who has, to this point, looked out for him as no other adult male has. And Twain, as bold as an author can be, takes over. For perhaps the first time in American literature, Jim, a black man, tells Huck off dramatically. Remembering this is being written just 20 years after the Emancipation Proclamation when much of America was not exactly receptive to this idea, the reader marvels at Twain's courage. Or should.

After explaining how close to despair he was worrying about the lost Huck, Jim concludes his moving passage this way: "Dat truck dah is *trash*; en trash is what people is dat puts dirt on de head er dey fren's en makes 'em ashamed."

Reading this aloud in class, one by one, I could see their eyes come up from the text to focus on me. Yes, this is a big deal. Twenty years or so before the Civil War, black men did not talk back, much less criticize a white person, and I made sure my students understood that. But now, Twain goes further. He has Huck do what any reasonable, moral person

2. A Rich Tapestry of Themes

would and should do in such a situation: apologize. And with the weight of pre-war Southern society on his shoulders, it isn't easy: "It was fifteen minutes," Huck tells us, "before I could work myself up to go and humble myself to a nigger—but I done it, and I warn't ever sorry for afterwards, neither."

The classroom was silent. The emotion in the air was palpable. "Imagine a Civil War veteran, and there were plenty of them around then, reading that?" I asked. "Imagine someone from Alabama or Mississippi, some place still very bitter about the defeat in the Civil War reading that, wondering if maybe someday, they'd have to apologize to a, well...."

To me, this is where some critics misconstrue what Twain is doing in this novel, "N" word or no "N" word. When we finished this scene and began to discuss it, there was a look of realization, or maybe even a secret thrill in the eyes that stared back at me across my classroom. Ah, their looks seemed to say, there *were* white writers, even back then, who stood up for African-Americans, writers who dared to call white America on its awful, inhuman treatment of black people.

Finding that moment when Huck's unfailing conscience steers him to the morally, if not socially correct decision to stick up for Jim, Twain had my students then. I could see it in their faces. I was starting to see it in their assignments: "I was surprised when Huck apologized," one student wrote. "White people didn't apologize to black people back then, I don't think. So when Huck did, I think it was hard for him. But he knew it was the right thing to do. And it *was* the right thing to do." For a 10th grader to arrive at that conclusion, I think, shows Twain's effectiveness in revealing Huck's character. And that his recognition of Jim's humanity, revealed in beautiful moments like this, is not some small thing.

Near the end of the long chapter sixteen, now that Twain has us—and Huck—enthralled in this dilemma: what do I do with Jim? It is a potent mix: the humor of chapter fourteen, Huck's moral awakening in chapter fifteen and now, the look-in-the-mirror realization of Huck, who believes that *he* is responsible for what's going on. As he says, "Jim said it made him all over trembly and feverish to be so close to freedom. Well, I can you it made me all over trembly and feverish, too to hear him, because I begun to get it through my head that he *was* most free—and who was to blame for it Why, *me*."

Now, of course, Huck isn't really at fault. It was Jim's decision to run away. But because Southern society had decreed that anyone who does not turn in a runaway slave is a lawbreaker, Huck's conscience begins to peck at him. And wonderfully, every time Twain has Jim shout out "Dah's Cairo" we feel the dagger of guilt in Huck's back and at the same time, also how tormented he is because he likes and cares for and respects Jim.

As Huck listens to Jim open his heart—probably the only white person he'd ever confided anything to—and explain how he wants to get his family back together, he begins to talk boldly and (for the time) disrespectfully, Huck begins to wonder if he'd created a nightmare for himself: "He wouldn't ever dared to talk such talk in his life before," Huck says after hearing Jim explain his plans. "Just see what difference it made in him the minute he judged he was about free. It was according to the old saying 'Give a nigger an inch and he'll take an ell.'" So, again, Huck is driven by what he feels in the pressure of Southern society and not knowing how to rationalize this, decides to go turn Jim in. As readers, we get the sense Huck has nowhere else to turn. He can't live with himself if he lets it go. But saying that, he's tormented because of how he feels about Jim.

It's an emotional scene and Twain crafts it beautifully. Huck decides to take the canoe to go turn Jim in. Jim, sensing Huck is about to betray him, puts his own jacket down for Huck to sit on (clever move). Then, the killer line: "Dah you goes, de ole true Huck; de on'y white genlman dat ever kep' his promise to ole Jim." By this time, I could see the class change. These three consecutive chapters hooked them. They knew Huck, they knew Jim and, of course, they were rooting hard for Jim to get to freedom.

In teaching this chapter, I almost always stop after Jim's comment and ask my class exactly that question: "What should Huck do here?" Since the *Mark Twain Tonight* clip I showed the class early on concludes with this very scene, as we read it in the classroom, I could see the recognition of this moment in some of their eyes. They didn't want him to turn in Jim, their ancestor. Huck doesn't want to turn Jim in, either. You feel the moment here. When, after sixteen chapters and a hundred or so pages, Huck gets his big chance, he chickens out. And we aren't disappointed, even if he is. Or says he is.

We understand, as readers, that he will be wrestling with this crisis again. A classroom full of African-American students felt Huck's torment in this moment. Particularly when Huck runs into trouble and is confronted by a skiff with two armed men looking for runaway slaves, Huck's quick thinking saves him once again. Huck puts on a marvelous acting performance, playing the role of the long, suffering young boy adrift on

2. A Rich Tapestry of Themes

the water with a dad who has contracted the then-deadly smallpox, something he knows will send them a-scurrying, which it does. They even give Huck $20 to try to get help for him and his ailing family, which was quite a haul back then. I also tried to explain the unwritten code of the river, an obligation to help anyone else in need. We talked about whether that sense of obligation still exists.

When Huck returns to the raft, Jim is in the water, hiding. He's tremendously appreciative of Huck, of course. But they don't talk much. You sense that Huck is still wrestling with—and maybe regretting—his decision, which is a neat trick for the author to pull off. As a reader, you sense he's not done with this issue.

3

A Splash, a Split and a Pause

One of the more recent developments in the reconstruction of the writing history of Mark Twain and *Huckleberry Finn* was the discovery of the other half of the manuscript in a California attic. Through the years, scholars have put together a probable timeline for the author's work on this novel and it appears that after splitting Huck and Jim with the incident with the steamboat, he wasn't sure how to proceed.

It may simply have been his instinct, since having put Huck and Jim through all this in the three succeeding chapters, the author made a momentous decision: split them up. Why? Here's a great question for your students, and really, for you. Why, having put the two of them through this miraculous and novel-changing stretch, break them apart? Why would an author do this? The students had lots of ideas: "Keeps the suspense," one said. "As a reader, like, I want to know if they're going to get back together?" "Two stories," added another. "Now you have two stories, where is Huck going, where is Jim going?" "Or what about this?" asked a third. "If he keeps the two of them on the raft, they've gotta talk about what just happened and whether Huck is guilty of anything and all that stuff. By separating them, each character has some time to think about what just happened and they don't have, you know, to try and figure it all out. That's not going to be easy."

All are good ideas. There's one other element: danger. If it's dangerous for a teenager like Huck to try to make his way on the river, what about a runaway slave? How will Jim get by? Will they catch him? Like the giant steamboat that smashed their raft and sent them tumbling into the big muddy, a giant wave spirals the novel forward. The supreme irony is that was where Twain stopped.

As Holbrook explains in the Ken Burns' special, Twain's creativity hit a sandbar: "He started to write this thing and he must have run into diffi-

3. *A Splash, a Split and a Pause*

culty," Holbrook explains. "He stops the book, puts it aside for five years. Then in April, 1882, he decides to go down the river to New Orleans on a steamboat to write another book, *Life On The Mississippi*. Then in May, he starts back up the river, again, all the way to Minnesota. And at the tag end of that, he visits Hannibal again. The next month, what does he do? He picks up *Huckleberry Finn* again. "What does that say to you?" Holbrook continues intensely. "What did he see going down that river. He'd been off that river for 20 years. Since before the Civil War. What do you think he was looking at? He was looking at the horrible failure of freeing the slave."

In "The United States of Huck," Saunders explains it in a slightly unusual way:

> All those adjustments (in Twain's plan) took place in part because his book was making him uncomfortable. His comic novel was doing things a comic novel was not supposed to do, and yet he sort of liked it, and come to think of it, it was really pretty darn uncomfortable but he didn't yet feel like fighting the battles his story was waging. In effect, his subconscious was urging him to do things his conscious mind didn't know could be done ... this tension between the various warring parts of Sam Clemens/Mark Twain—the radical and the reactionary; the savage satirist and friendly Humorist; the raw hick and the aspiring genteel Literary figure—is what makes *Huck Finn* such a rich and formidable book.

When he resumed writing—we know when Twain resumed the novel because he kept good notes on his work habits—the novel took a more sociological tone. Twain lands Huck smack in the middle of feud between the Shepherdsons and the Grangerfords, and for two dazzling chapters, Twain conjures up a friendship between Huck and Buck (notice the sound-alike ... implying this could-have-been Huck) that is perfect. You can see the two of them, fast friends already, and Buck finally getting someone his age, someone he could relate to, and Huck finding someone like Tom, a pal.

Not only that, but Huck finally has a home he's comfortable with. A home that he describes in such pains-taking detail, you know how much it impresses him. Twain's extraordinarily detailed description of this classy, genteel home serves another ironic purpose when you consider the family that populates this well-attended Southern home, seemingly the height of Southern society, is also engaged in a bloody, senseless feud with the Shepherdsons, a silly turf war. But before we learn too much about the repercussions of the feud, Huck also introduces us to Buck's late sister, Emmeline Grangerford, perhaps the first real "Goth" in American Literature.

Teaching *Huckleberry Finn*

Her tragically dark drawings and morbid topics make for some fun reading. Then comes Huck's astute comment that clinches it: "Everybody was sorry she died, because she had laid out a lot more of these pictures to do, and a body could see by what she had done what they had lost. But I reckoned, that with her disposition, she was having a better time in the graveyard." We also get a chance to hear her great Steven Dowling Bots poem, an ode to a guy who drowned in a well. It's hilarious stuff. I always make it a point to have several of my students read Twain's doggerel "in honor of Emmeline."

But just as in *Hamlet* when Shakespeare gets you laughing, you know something dreadful is about to happen, and so it is with Twain. After Buck narrowly escapes being shot by a Shepherdson and Huck finds out that the Grangerford's servants have hidden Jim, the lovely Miss Sophia enlists an unwitting Huck to send a message to the other side, the Shepherdsons (HE doesn't realize this, of course). When Sophia elopes with one of them, an all-out war ensues, and with Huck caught in a tree looking on in horror, his friend Buck is shot and killed. When we get to this moment in class— it always is silent, respectful and sad. I usually ask one of my students to read Huck's lines. You can usually hear their voice tremble a little: "When I got down out of the tree, I crept along down the river bank a piece, and found the two bodies laying in the edge of the water, and tugged at them till I got them ashore; then I covered up their faces, and got away as quick as I could. I cried a little when I was covering up Buck's face, for he was mighty good to me." Not for the first time, death has touched Huck Finn. And, really, our class, too. This great adventure Huck has been on, it doesn't seem so great. He's scared. And should be. This world that he seemed to be breezing through has come to a halt. Is he next?

Twain, of course, has the answer. Jim is just waiting with the raft and the two of them escape, leaving the utterly uncivilized civilized life behind them, heading for the peace and contentment of open water.

Almost as if his prose were music and he wanted to calm things down, Twain's opening to Chapter nineteen is tranquil, glorious and often quoted. It clearly is some of Twain's most beautifully descriptive and poetic writing. We really get a sense of Twain's years on the river, what life was like for him as a riverboat pilot and his extraordinary sensibilities. It's a brilliant example of nature writing, someone who not only was there but also can bring it back to us as if we were standing right next to him.

After we've read it, I always like to note that Twain dropped out of

3. A Splash, a Split and a Pause

school as a youngster, a long way from what we now call high school. Does he write like a dropout? Goes to show you what you can do with talent—and drive. When we get to this place, I always put the lights down in class—just bright enough for me to read. Then I ask them to do one thing, which is listen:

> It was a monstrous big river down there- sometimes a mile and a half wide; we run nights, and laid up and hid day-times; soon as night was most gone, we stopped navigating and tied up- nearly always in the dead water under a towhead; and then cut young cottonwoods and willows and hid the raft with them. Then we set out the lines. Next we slid into the river and had a swim, so as to freshen up and cool off; then we set down on the sandy bottom where the water was about knee deep, and watched the daylight come. Not a sound, anywheres- perfectly still- just like the whole world was asleep, only sometimes the bull-frogs a-cluttering, maybe. The first thing to see, looking away over the water, was a kind of dull line- that was the woods on t'other side- you couldn't make nothing else out; then a pale place in the sky; then more paleness, spreading around; then the river softened up, away off, and warn't black any more, but gray; you could see little dark spots drifting along, ever so far away-trading scows, and such things; and long black streaks- rafts; sometimes you could hear a sweep screaking; or jumbled up voices, it was so still, and sounds come so far; and by-and-by you could see a streak on the water which you know by the look of the streak that there's a snag there in a swift current which breaks on it and makes that streak look that way; and you see the mist curl up off of the water, and the east reddens up, and the river, and you make out a log cabin in the edge of the woods, away on the bank on t'other side of the river, being a wood-yard, likely, and piled by them cheats so you can throw a dog through it anywheres; then the nice breeze blows up, and comes fanning you from over there, so cool and fresh, and sweet to smell, on account of the woods and the flowers; but sometimes not that way, because they've left dead fish laying around, gars, and such, and they do get pretty rank; and next you've got the full day, and everything smiling in the sun, and the song-birds just going it!

You can see from their faces, they are there with Huck, on the edge of the raft, kicking their feet in the cool Mississippi.

Just when it seems as if Huck and Jim have cleared things out for a good run on the river—haven't they had enough excitement for a while?—here comes two more from Twain's never-ending carnival of characters. The king and the duke, two con men chased by a pack of barking dogs and angry men, hop aboard Huck and Jim's raft just as the two are heading for open water. Semi-professional actors (that may be a stretch), they quickly concoct an amazing story for Huck and Jim, one so ridiculous (they are related to French royalty) neither Huck nor Jim know what to say. Truthfully, with Huck fearful of Jim being exposed and himself implicated, the pair are more gracious than they should be and the scoundrels settle in. For a while, these two hijack the book, giving us additional illustrations of man's inhumanity to man. They are con men, of course: one young, one old, full of half-understood Shakespeare and the nerve to pull anything on anybody to make a buck. What each one did understand was the sure sense of the swindle and neither one had an ounce of shame.

For a while, Huck and Jim aren't quite sure what to make of their stories and claims—except to doubt every other word. Since he has some explaining of his own to do (Jim?), Huck decides that he'll keep quiet. "If I never learnt nothing else out of Pap," he confides in us, "I learnt that the best way to get along with his kind of people is to let them have their own way." Which they do. Claiming to be actors, the two crooks put on a Shakespeare skit called the Royal Nonesuch, earn $87.75 on a one-night stop ashore and return to the raft with a handbill depicting a runaway slave with a $200 reward printed on it. "Now," says the duke, "after tonight, we can run in the daytime if we want to. Whenever we see anybody coming, we can tie Jim hand and foot with a rope, and lay him in the wigwam and show this handbill and say we captured him up the river, and were too poor to travel on a steamboat, so we got this little raft on credit from our friends and going down to get the reward."

If, as a reader, you're getting the idea that this isn't going to end well, you're right. Once again, Twain has written his duo into what you might call a raft of trouble. As morally bankrupt white men with potent information—Jim is a runaway slave—they have an ace in the hole, you might say. While it's certainly clear they can't be trusted, they're on the run; it's not as if they can do anything with this information. But they will. So, it's good to note here that the built-in tension of taking a runaway slave down the Mississippi River has just been, oh, doubled?

For the next stretch, chapters twenty-one through twenty-four, Twain entertains us as the king and duke entertain Huck and Jim—with a little bit of cornball Shakespeare, including what you might call a frontier version of Hamlet. It's the kind of on-the-raft distraction to lure us away from his real purpose here, which is to continue to plumb Huck's sensitive soul. A teaching point here: as we looked at these chapters, I explained to my students that to me, one of the great and unexpected strengths of the book is how Twain manages to find other ways of making the reader root for Huck, alone in what seems to be a corrupt world.

3. A Splash, a Split and a Pause

For example, in chapter twenty-one, he has Huck go into town. It's a common enough idea for a kid who's been stuck on a raft, traveling by night for weeks now. But Twain turns Huck's visit into something else. Once in town, Huck witnesses a harmless old drunk by the name of Boggs, weaving through town at midday. Full of bad whiskey and false bravado, Boggs makes what turns out to be the fatal mistake of insulting a Colonel Sherburn, a dignified man who has no time for drunks. Considering Huck's past (Pap?) he knows about drunks and how ugly that can be. But when Boggs ignores Sherburn's warning, speaks disrespectfully once more, everyone is stunned to see Sherburn gun him down in cold blood, just for having insulted him. Suddenly, the raft seems like the place to be. This scene, and the aftermath—a lynch mob charges to Sherburn's house where he stands them down, well, it's one of Twain's most powerfully written set pieces. Sometimes in his one-man *Mark Twain Tonight* show, Holbrook will dramatize this scene in spectacular fashion.

For my students, teaching this scene about a senseless shooting, where someone dies because of someone's pride (or fear), they had no trouble drawing a parallel to real life, whether that current case happens to be in Minnesota or Missouri. Though someone could have stepped in and stopped what turned out to be murder, nobody did.

When the mob storms Sherburn's house seeking retribution in chapter twenty-two, Sherburn calls them on their collective cowardice in another powerfully drawn scene. This has the ring of authenticity to it, something that Twain likely witnessed in his time in the west, a moment where he saw humanity for what it was. Seeing death first-hand shapes Huck, changes him, and as readers, we roll along with him, a little bit wiser, a little bit sadder.

While Huck may be wiser and sadder, he's still a kid. When he gets a chance to sneak in to the circus, Huck is enthralled and, to our relief, sounds like it came at just the right time. "It was a real bully circus," he says, "It was the splendidest sight that ever was when they all come riding in, two and two, a gentleman and lady, side by side, the men just in their drawers and undershirts, and no shoes nor stirrups, and resting their hands on their thighs easy and comfortable—the must a been twenty of them—every lady with a lovely complexion, and perfectly beautiful, and looking just like a gang of real sure-enough queens, and dressed in clothes that cost millions of dollars, and just littered with diamonds. It was a powerful fine sight; I never see anything so lovely." As the events of the circus unfold and a drunk rider manages to convince the ring master to do a trick, he begins to do what appears to be a stunt that grows more dangerous with every spin around the big top. The crowd is going wild; they love the idea that something awful might happen and they are there to see it. But Huck, kind soul that he is, why, he's almost deathly frightened for him: "It warn't funny to me, though," he says. "I was all of a tremble to see his danger."

It turns out to be a stunt, a marvelously concocted trick with an expert rider, who has the crowd going wild by the end of his ride. By including it, Twain gently reminds us that despite all Huck's seen and gone through, he's still just a kid who is easily swayed and, as shown here, not someone who goes along with the crowd. For me, this is an opportunity to quiz the kids about inference, how, though Twain never comes right out and says it, we are reminded of Huck's age and gullibility and compassion. And just as Huck truly feared for that trick rider, we fear for him, knowing the king and duke have something in store for he and Jim, too.

At this point, the reader expects there's more sad news ahead for each one; they can feel it. What the reader doesn't expect at the end of chapter twenty-three is one more heart-wrenching nugget from Jim, who shares his guilt with Huck over unfairly punishing his daughter, Elizabeth, who had lost her hearing to scarlet fever, unbeknownst to her father. As Jim wails to his young friend, "O Huck, I bust out a-cryin,' en grab her up in my arms en say, 'O de po' little thing! de Lord God Almighty forgive po' ole Jim, kaze he never gwyne to forgive hisself as long's he live! O she was plumb deef en dumb, plum deef en dumb—en I'd been a-treat'n her so." As with the scene with Buck's death, the classroom went silent, imagining the silent torment of that little girl and her father.

With the king and duke carrying on, in chapter twenty-four, Twain tosses in a nifty little demonstration of the king and the duke in action—on the con. After posting a sign that describes Jim as a "sick Arab" in case anyone comes snooping around, they dress up and head into town and take a brief steamboat ride just to see if they can scare up some more money. Sure enough, an innocent, trusting visitor spills his soul to the king, explaining that the death of Peter Wilks is sure to bring his two brothers, *wealthy* brothers, to town for the funeral at the home of the Wilks' sisters, and the dispensing of the will. After this unsuspecting young man gets a thorough grilling from the king, who gets himself the full back story so he can use it to his advantage and you know why. See if your stu-

3. *A Splash, a Split and a Pause*

dents will get it. What's coming next? Before you can say or spell "swindle," you can see what's going to happen, can't you? It's a good little writing exercise, just to see if the class is onto Twain's idea. What do you think will happen next, class? Explain...

Sure enough, as chapter twenty-four ends, the "actors" put on a show that you can turn into a fun classroom skit as the king and duke "meet" their long-lost relatives, the king affecting the phoniest of British accents:

"...when we got to the village they yawled us ashore. About two dozen men flocked down when they see the yawl-a-coming, and when the king says: "Kin any of you gentlemen tell me wher' Mr. Peter Wilks lives?" they give a glance at one another, and nodded their heads, as much as to say, "What d' I tell you?" Then one of them says, kind of soft and gentle: "I'm sorry, sir, but the best we can do is tell you where he DID live yesterday evening." Sudden as winking the ornery old creetur went an to smash, and fell up against the man, and put his chin on his shoulder, and cried down his back, and says: "Alas, alas, our poor brother—gone, and we never got to see him; oh, it's too, too hard!"

Then he turned around, blubbering, and makes a lot of idiotic signs to the duke on his hands, and blamed if he didn't drop a carpet-bag and bust out a-crying. If they warn't the beatenest lot, them two frauds, that ever I struck. Well, the men gathered around and sympathized with them, and said all sorts of kind things to them, and carried their carpet-bags up the hill for them, and let them lean on them and cry, and told the king all about his brother's last moments, and the king her told it all over again on his hands to the duke, and both of them took on about that dead tanner like they'd lost the twelve disciples. Well, if ever I struck anything like it, I'm a nigger. It was enough to make a body ashamed of the human race.

4

Twain Stops the Show—
As Intended

After the chicanery of chapter twenty-four when we, as readers, may begin to doubt the nature of humanity, Twain gives us a moment for all-time. In Huck's dealing with the king and duke, he's exposed to the worst of our world. And, as an eyewitness to their thievery and moral bankruptcy—legally, couldn't Huck be an accomplice?—this episode seems to flick a switch for him. Can he stand there and watch this? What is his moral obligation, even if he is a kid? He feels it, and as readers, we feel it, too. This is an interesting moment here, one that, if you stop and think about it, raises all kinds of questions about obligation, society, a citizen's duty, etc.

When we got to this point, I brought up a couple of seemingly unrelated concepts that we explored earlier in the class. The first one goes along with a famous Ray Bradbury short story and episode from HBO's "The Ray Bradbury Theater" called "Marionettes, Inc." where a man trapped in an unhappy marriage buys a robot to do his daily duties for him so he can go and play. But the moment early in the story that we focus on is when the unhappy man asks the company why they are doing this. When the president of the company explains that any human being has the right, and the duty to interfere if he sees a fellow member of the species about to go off a cliff, we paused here to discuss. If you had a friend who's doing something that's dangerous or illegal or just plain dumb, would you be obligated to say something? "None of my business," one student said. "I don't want nobody messing in my business." "But if you're a friend," I counter. "Wouldn't you want someone to help you if you were heading in a bad direction?" "Maybe," another student agreed. "But how do you know when you aren't sticking your nose in?" "These are all good questions," I

4. Twain Stops the Show—As Intended

said, and I could see they were all thinking about this. When should you speak up? Is your friendship worth speaking up for? That's a good question and they looked around at one another. What is friendship, anyway? Only someone to hang around with when things are going good? Shouldn't you be there for the hard times, too?

After we talked about that, I brought up the other point, about your moral obligation. This was an issue, oddly enough, that the Seinfeld finale tackled, something we had talked about earlier in the year. The four of them are witnesses to a robbery, a rather large, helpless individual is robbed, and they do nothing but make fun of how fat the guy is and laugh about his plight.

Later, they are arrested for failing to do anything: the new "Good Samaritan" law. Then came a lengthy trial where everyone that they had wronged, one way or another over the nine years of the show came back and told how awful they were. Nobody seemed to really like the ambitious Seinfeld finale but that question, what are you obligated to do in that type of situation, is a good one. Is it ok to just look away, to not try and do something? This is really where Huck is. He knows these scoundrels are about to hoodwink these people and it'll be on his conscience. And that's where Twain is going.

For me, in my demographic area, this is an important lesson. Because when we see poor behavior or bad decision-making, there always seems to be somebody making excuses for them because of their home situation or past issues. You can't be a teacher in our setting and not acknowledge that, but at the same time, I don't excuse it.

There may be no logical reason that Huck has the moral code he does; let's face it, there are all kinds of excuses out there for him if he turns out bad: Pap is a drunk, he doesn't have a mom, he was raised in horrible circumstances, and he's almost illiterate. But Huck does not do that. Maybe that's one reason why, in my school, where so many of my students are growing up in less-than desirable circumstances, I wanted them to see you can do it. Huck did. So can you.

Having had a front-row seat to all of the king and the duke's dishonesty to the sweet, trusting Wilks' girls, Huck determines he has to do something for them. He lays in bed, "feeling ornery and low down and mean" and decides, in a brief passage that brilliantly and maturely analyzes the situation, the only thing he can do is steal their coming inheritance, the $6,000, so the king and duke don't get it. In snooping around to find the loot, he overhears the king and the depth of his depravity: "What! And not sell out the rest o' the property?" he says. "March off like a passel o' fools and leave eight or nine thous'n dollars' worth o' property layin' around jest sufferin' to be scooped in?—and all good saleable stuff, too." Huck knows what this means. They're not just taking the bag of gold; they're out for everything. So he has to do it now, and carefully, he does. He steals the money and, stuck for a place to hide it, puts it in Peter Wilks' coffin.

Good ol' Huck. When he explains everything to Mary Jane, where the money is hidden and how everything will work out, she begins to tear up and says to Huck, "'Goodbye—I'm going to do everything just as you've told me; and if I don't ever see you again, I shan't ever forget you, and I'll think of you a many and a many a time, and I'll *pray* for you, too!'—and she was gone." Then Huck slays, he really does, with his next lines: "Pray for me! I reckoned if she knowed me she'd take a job that was more nearer her size. But I bet she done it; just the same—she was just that kind. She had the grit to pray for Judus if she took the notion..." He thinks he's bad, when he's really good. It's a theme Twain will continue to use brilliantly throughout the novel.

After Huck and Jim nearly escape without the two scoundrels at the end of chapter twenty-nine, Twain gives us a bit of low comedy—the king and duke arguing about who put the bag of money in the coffin. Again, this is ripe for a fun classroom mini-play, as Twain not only displays their hollow souls but also registers how far Huck is from them, even given his background. We still expect, as readers, that they aren't about to waste their opportunity with a runaway slave, and here, they act on it.

When Huck finally breaks away on their trip to town, he returns to an empty raft. He is alone, truly. And here, he has us and we have him—in our hearts. Think of a 12-year-old boy who's already been through more than he could ever tell (why not write a book?) and now he not only has to somehow get rid of the king and the duke, he must find, then probably free, Jim. We say probably because although they are close, Huck has been taught and believes it is wrong for him to be helping Jim. He knows what people will say, how he likely will be treated if they found out; he's unsettled. We all would be.

When he gets back on the road, he at least gets some information that he needs. Jim is at Silas Phelps' place, he's told. The king sold him for 40 dollars: "Forty dirty dollars," Huck calls it. And when he gets back to the raft, he thinks about how low-down the king and the duke—white

4. Twain Stops the Show—As Intended

adults, remember—really are: "After all this long journey, and after all we'd done for them scoundrels, here was it all come to nothing, everything all busted up and ruined, because they could have heart to serve Jim such a trick as that, and make him a slave again all his life, and amongst strangers, too, for forty dirty dollars." The phrase, so well chosen, sticks with us. It feels right; it stings us, as it must have Huck. And here, after all these adventures and characters and laughs and tears, Twain has brought his young narrator to the brink. Here he is, alone on a raft somewhere in the Deep South, wrestling with a problem that one way or another is going to change his life. What should he do? Should he try and free Jim? That's what we, as readers, want him to do, and reading this passage in class, I could surely tell that's what the kids wanted to happen. How could he pull this off? Stealing money from a bunch of charlatans was one thing. But freeing a man, by himself, well, that's something else again. And is that what he *should* do? Society certainly says no, hell, no. But he can't just walk away. His extraordinary heart and the bond he has with Jim won't let that happen. We sense it.

It is an extraordinary moment in American literature. It is the second and final time Huck will deal with this issue and it stops the show, as is completely intended. His head and a nation's morals all point in one direction. His heart, though, says something else. In powerful, soul-scraping writing, Huck plumbs his soul.

Guilty over the whole mess with Jim, Huck isn't sure what to do. In desperation, he writes a letter to Miss Watson, then decides to rip it up. His decision will ultimately shape the rest of the book. He decides, with extraordinary courage, that he's going to try and free Jim. And if he goes to Hell for it, so be it. I always read this page aloud. The passage is so powerful, Huck's ruminations so honest and thoughtful and probing, you can't help but be drawn in. Sometimes, I even find my own voice cracking. Though this moment didn't seem to impress some critics, every one of my classes stops cold at this scene. I always stress, again and again, that Huck truly thinks he is going to Hell for his decision to help a black man, yet he does it because it's the right thing to do. What a great lesson for high schoolers. And it connected. There were smiles all around, and not just because someone said "Hell" in a classroom. Extraordinary writer that he is, Twain puts us in Huck's head as he sits and ponders this momentous decision, clearly the most important one he'll ever make in his life, the only decision, we know by now, that the whole book is aimed at.

Teaching *Huckleberry Finn*

What now seems incredible to me—and I've done a fair amount of research on this—is that America *did not get it*. As Andrew Levy explains in his valuable *Huck Finn's America*, we did not see what Twain was doing at all. The author's purpose was hiding in plain sight: "Virtually no surviving review of the book, and there are dozens, talks about the novel as if it were bringing anything new to the story of black and white in America. And those few references thought what Twain said on the subject was *funny*. "Most amusing," wrote the *Hartford Courant*, "is the struggle Huck has with his conscience in regard to slavery." "In the Southern newspapers, *Huck* was almost invisible. "Possibly Mark Twain's later novels are coarse and dime-novelish," wrote the *Augusta Chronicle & Constitutionalist* in March 1885. "We do not know. We have not read them." "In the black newspapers, Twain *was* invisible, and his book seemingly ignored."

As we read it now, we wonder how they could have missed the boat, the dock, and the pier. It seems so clear, as Lance Morrow explains in his essay, "Huck Finn and Censorship," what Twain is trying to do: "Huck's two-page struggle over whether to betray Jim in a masterpiece of metaphysically comic inversion, a sardonic, hilarious examination of conscience," he writes. "Huck accuses himself of low-down, ornery wickedness "in stealing a poor old woman's nigger." The law—righteousness, the society's definition of good—says Huck is doing an awful thing in harboring Jim. Huck tries to pray, but "my heart warn't right." At last, Huck decides he cannot turn in his friend, Jim. In one of the great moments in American literature, Huck says, "All right, then, I'll go to hell." He has done the loneliest, bravest work there is—facing a life-or-death decision against the law and custom of his own tribe. In the Ken Burns' segment on *Huck*, novelist Russell Banks affirms its power: "That sentence, it makes the hair on the back of my neck stand up today, when I think about that sentence. It's a great moral awakening for White Americans. There is then the possibility of redemption (for our great sin, slavery.)"

In moments like this, when I looked into the young eyes staring back at me, as they imagined some crusty old white guy, peering through a cloud of cigar smoke in his little alcove on a New York hillside, writing words that even now, can affect black people like a loving pat on the back, the whitest of white guys sticking up for them, you ought to see their smiles, their heads nodding. I think it's from moments like this one that enabled some of my students to feel and write as though Twain was a long-lost friend from long ago, someone they never met but wished they had.

4. Twain Stops the Show—As Intended

With a class like mine, you didn't have to explain the courage that Twain showed by writing this, by making Jim, unlettered and uneducated as he may have been, the actual hero of the book. They've grown up in a world not unlike Huck's, most of them. There haven't been a lot of people white people on their side. But here's one. And yes, there's hope.

Huck now has a plan. He wants to find Jim and set him free. He needs to find him, deal with the lingering effects of the king and the duke, which he does brilliantly, and bring the novel home. What to do?

5

Navigating His Way to the Finish

As we head into the closing chapters, this is where we took a moment, as a class, and discussed what we thought should happen, what we expected to happen and what does happen. In a novel like this, where we've seen characters dragged through so much, we recognize the ending is going to be complicated. In real life, we recognize also that it's very possible, if not probable, that Jim will not be set free or that Huck will be punished for what he did. No matter how good, how respectful, how downright solid Jim was in every aspect, to just about everybody else around then, he was property. They weren't about to let him go because he was kind to a runaway. Twain makes it clear that Huck is running some considerable risk trying to get his friend free. How, as an author, can he steer through this deep, dark water, even with his riverboat captain experience? How can he navigate his way home?

If you were Twain, sitting in that little gazebo, maybe you're thinking to yourself, well, freeing a slave might be a bit much for one kid to tackle. Especially one that had seen the death and treachery all around that Huck had. Maybe he needs help. Now, this has been a much-debated authorial decision over the years. To some, including no less an author than Ernest Hemingway, bringing Tom Sawyer back into the story was a gaffe. Sawyer and his silly imaginings had been dismissed by Huck earlier in the novel with his withering crack about all Sawyer's silly "julery and a-rabs" that Sunday afternoon. With a delightful air of nonchalance, Huck surveys the scene and blows it away: "It had all the marks of a Sunday school," Huck mutters disgustedly. Yet that said, if you think about a 12-year-old boy, sitting alone in the wigwam on the raft, wouldn't he like some help? Wouldn't he, if he'd been granted this wish, asked for Tom Sawyer to come and help him?

5. Navigating His Way to the Finish

There has been so much written about this over the years by all sorts of writers. But I've never seen one suggest that if Huck had had a cell phone, wouldn't he have texted Tom, wherever he was and said, "Hey, dude, come help me with this." We'll never know, of course, what convinced Twain, nearing the end of what was a very difficult novel for him, to bring back Tom Sawyer. And how he did it, well, writers all over the world would like to be let in on that secret: "Let's see, I'll have Jim go to a farm that's owned by Tom Sawyer's *aunt* and I'll have *Tom Sawyer* just *happen* to visit and together, the two of them will get Jim out and I believe I'll go have me a drink of whiskey..."

As George Saunders explains in his wonderful Introduction, Twain is really pushing his authorial luck here in his passage titled "The Ending, Oh My God, the Ending":

> So what does Twain do? This literary purist, who had lambasted James Fenimore Cooper for his too-lengthy canoes and exaggeratedly hearing-gifted Indians, commits one of the worst Coincidences in the history of writing. Huck approaches the house where Jim is being held, planning to enact another swindle, and a woman comes out, mistakes him for another little boy (we flinch a bit at this; mistaken identity has been used maybe once too often in this book), and then—horror of horrors—we learn that this other little boy's name is Tom, and we begin whispering to ourselves, No way, no way, Mark, Sam—don't do it—but our worst fears are soon confirmed: this woman is Tom Sawyer's aunt, and she—here, eleven hundred miles upriver—is expecting a visit from Tom himself any minute now.
>
> Now, a coincidence is all right, life is full of them, but a reader's willingness to ingest one is inversely related to how badly the writer needs one, and Twain needed one very badly at this point, to avoid stepping into the dangerous trap his subconscious had set for him.

As a reader, a writer and a teacher, I agree that Saunders and many others make a very valid, hard-to-argue point. Talk about far-fetched. But in seven years of teaching the novel, I've yet to hear a *single* objection, a smirk or any sort of dismissive talk. Granted, I'm dealing with high school readers. It would be interesting to measure how a college class, one not versed in the controversy, would respond to Twain's ending.

So as not to spoil anything for my classes, I never discuss the controversy over the ending until after we've finished the book, in the same way you wouldn't want Roger Ebert to come into your house, stop the DVD in the middle and say, "You know, a lot of people said this ending really sucked. I can't believe you're still watching this."

Teaching *Huckleberry Finn*

At least so far, they certainly seemed to be buying Twain's amazing coincidence to close out the novel; that Jim *just happens* to be held on a farm owned by *Tom Sawyer's aunt* and *Tom is on his way for a visit, to help Huck—and Twain—end the novel?* Maybe it's the Harry Potter/Hunger Games Generation, where the logic and common sense that us adults think will kick in, doesn't. They don't question the author's motive and are mostly just anxious to see if, finally, Jim will get his freedom. Very often, right here I'll give them an impromptu in-class writing assignment. What next? Based on what you've read so far, what should happen?

I've always found it a great exercise to have your students write out what they *expect* to happen, where the story's headed. Or, once a story is completed, have your students add another page or two, extend the story, and answer the question, where do they think the author was leading us? To do that, they have to think about the characters, how the original author ended his story and what that all means. It's all implication, reading the tealeaves. I certainly never had a teacher ask me that in the middle of a story. I wish they had.

What we as readers want—and especially my classes—is a) for Jim to be freed and b) for he and Huck to keep on going down that river, having adventures and stopping time—that whole annoying idea of growing up and facing the poisonous hatred that will still be around in the summer of 2017, say.

Twain certainly understood that and his ending shows that. What perhaps he didn't understand was that he had evolved Huck to some degree past the racism of his time, that when we arrive at the dramatic finish, it would seem completely wrong to have Huck sort of weak-mindedly go along with Tom Sawyer's goofily and heartless idea of toying around with Jim's captivity. It seems like a step in the wrong direction, they say. Hasn't Huck just recognized Jim as a man and a friend? How can he listen to Tom Sawyer's nonsense after all they've been through together? And it clearly is *together*. Like Huck says, returning from one of his reconnaissance missions: "They're after us."

So, again ... how you approach teaching the ending is a matter of opinion. With a perhaps college-level group of students, I might have paused at this point and gotten into the various criticisms of the ending of the book before we go and read it. There is plenty to go into and it can help them understand things at a deeper level. But if you do that, you can detract from the novel's momentum and your class' desire to find out the

5. Navigating His Way to the Finish

resolution. There'll be time for discussion later. I recommend just plowing on through and letting Twain's last-minute revelations put a look of wonder on their face.

In chapter thirty-two, Huck is able to ditch the king and duke and find the Phelps' farm. And again, Twain finds a lovely way to discuss faith, in a subtle way. Understandably, Huck is scared, and it shows: "I went around and clumb over the back stile by the ash-hopper, and started for the kitchen. When I got a little ways, I heard the dim hum of a spinning wheel waiting along up and sinking along down again: and then I knowed for certain I wished I was dead—for that *is* the lonesomest sound in the whole world. I went right along, not fixing up any particular plan, but just trusting to Providence to put the right words in my mouth when the time come; for I'd noticed that Providence always did put the right words in my mouth, if I left it alone." Though he doesn't come out and say it, isn't admitting here he has a guardian angel, someone who looks out for him, someone who has looked out for him ever since he faked his death back with Pap all those miles ago? That paragraph is a famous quote from the novel; writers often cite it to display Huck's quick wit and adaptability, all of which are indisputable. But you can go deeper, further.

Another point I always remark to my students here is Twain's use of sensory details to heighten the drama and tension. Huck is sneaking up on the farm, which is dangerous enough. But to hear that eerie sound, to bring up the idea of death, which is something that very well could happen to him in that instant ... it's brilliant.

Delightfully, just as we're wondering what Huck and Providence are going to come up with—we're waiting—Twain flips the script. Aunt Sally Phelps spots him, "smiling all over so she could hardly stand—and says: 'It's *you*, at last!—*ain't it?*" How is Huck, a pleaser, particularly to women, going to deny that? His alibi is all set up; he must listen and react. He does, superbly, bringing us along with his train of thought, us wondering how he's going to respond before he does. And it's here that Twain finds another subtle but superb way to comment on race in another oft-quoted passage. Huck is explaining his delay and says, "It wasn't the grounding—that didn't keep us back but a little. We blowed out a cylinder-head." "Good gracious! Anybody hurt?" "No'm. Killed a nigger." Which is exactly, we think, the way a teenager would have explained it in 1840 or thereabouts. While we've had dozens of previous chapters or so to the contrary, Huck is code switching here, fitting in with the way the Phelps and others of that era

Teaching *Huckleberry Finn*

would have thought. The scene would work without that line, certainly. That Twain chose to include it speaks, again, to his overall authorial purpose.

And just as Aunt Sally's questioning has brought Huck to the brink of all-out confession or something, Twain's skillful hand at comedy comes in. Silas Phelps returns from a visit to pick up their intended visitor, Aunt Sally stashes Huck under a bed, gives ol' Silas the business for missing their visitor, and then pulls him out from under the bed, saying to an astonished Silas, "Who do you reckon 't is?" ... "It's *Tom Sawyer!*" Twain doesn't mention Providence here, but he could have. For we know what Huck does, he can talk all day and night about Tom Sawyer, Providence did come through for him again, and holy smokes, what is Tom Sawyer doing coming to visit? How will Huck—and Twain—handle that? As a writer, the plot almost propels itself.

When the two do meet on the road, momentarily, Twain has yet another little twist, one that sets up the finish. After Huck convinces Tom he's not a ghost—last time Tom looked for him, he was dead, remember—Huck shares an awful secret: "...there's a nigger here that I'm trying to steal out of slavery—and his name is *Jim*—old Miss Watson's Jim." Tom says: "What! Why Jim is—" "I know what you'll say," (blurts Huck, panicked thinking of what Tom might think of him). "You'll say it's dirty low-down business; but what if it is?—I'm low-down; and I'm agoing to steal him, and I want you to keep mum and not let on. Will you?" Now here, Twain has a surprise for Huck—and us, which sets up what happens at the close of the book perfectly: "His eye lit up, and he says: "I'll *help* you steal him!" Huck cannot believe what he has heard. And understanding the situation in that time period, we are surprised, too: "Well, I let go all holts, then, like I was shot. It was the most astonishing speech I ever heard—and I'm bound to say Tom Sawyer fell, considerable, in my estimation. Only I couldn't believe it. Tom Sawyer *a nigger stealer!*"

Twain's rich use of irony here lands hard. If we admire Huck for trying to free his friend and we feel his torment and shame, when he learns his best friend *is willing to pitch in* ... you know what Huck is thinking, even though Twain needn't come out and say it: now I'm *really* going to Hell.

As a teacher, this kind of close reading and inference makes for thoughtful discussion. It truly makes a young reader consider why a writer does this or that, what it means, how it interacts with what came before. More than just about any other book I've ever read, *Huckleberry Finn* offers these moments for you to share.

5. Navigating His Way to the Finish

Okay, so now Twain has Tom and Huck at the Phelps' plantation with Jim in captivity. We're wondering how they're going to get him out. But first, as only Twain can, a comic interlude. Tom arrives at the house, says his name is William Thompson, is welcomed heartily by one and all and then, "he reached over and kissed aunt Sally right on the mouth, then settled back again, in his chair, comfortable, and was going on talking; but she jumped up, wiped it off with the back of her hand, and says: "You owdacious puppy!" As readers, we are laughing, wondering where this will lead:

> "He looked kind of hurt, and says: 'I'm surprised at you, m'am.'
> 'You're s'rp—Why, what do you reckon I am? I've a good notion to take and—say, what do you mean by kissing me?'
> He looked kind of humble and says: 'I didn't mean nothing, m'am. I didn't mean no harm. I–I thought you'd like it.'
> 'Why, you born fool!' She took up the spinning-stick, and it looked like it was all she could do to keep from giving him a crack with it. 'What made you think I'd like it?'
> 'Well, I don't know. Only, they—they—told me you would.'
> '*They* told you I would. Whoever told you, 's *another* lunatic. I never heard the beat of it. Who's *they*?'

And it goes on until Tom (as his brother, Sid) wins the day by saying, "No'm. I'm honest about it. I won't ever do it again. 'Till you ask me." This scene, especially after all the heavy things that have come before, is sure to have your classroom like mine was—in stitches. Sex is not something alluded to very often in Twain's work, and with high school students, this little hint of it will always set them off.

Later that night, after Tom and Huck have snuck off and had a chance to catch up, Twain gives us a final glimpse of the scoundrels that sold Jim back into slavery and have done so much to dim Huck's view of the adult world. After this, he has no reason to change his thinking:

> ...here comes a raging rush of people, with torches, and an awful whooping yelling, and banging tin pans and blowing horns; and we jumped to one side to let them go by; and as they went by, I see they had the king and the duke astraddle of a rail—that is, I knowed it was the king and the duke, though they was all over tar and feather and didn't look like nothing in the world that was human—just looked like a couple monstrous big soldier-plumes. Well, it made me sick to see it; and I was sorry for them poor pitiful rascals, it seemed like I couldn't ever feel any hardness against them any more in the world. It was a dreadful thing to see. Human being *can* be awful cruel to one another.

Teaching *Huckleberry Finn*

If Huck has had doubts about religion to this point, organized religion anyway, his spirit here, the extraordinary breadth of his compassion, even after all the rotten things these characters did to he and Jim, he can't help but feel sorry for them, to pity them. Maybe, like Huck, I didn't learn my own religion right, but if that isn't a Christ-like attitude, well, I guess I read a different Bible.

Twain, however, goes a little bit further with this, again, plumbing Huck's boundless heart: "So, we poked along back home, and I warn't feeling so brash as I was before, but kind of ornery; and humble, and to blame, somehow—though *I* hadn't done nothing. But that's always the way; it don't make no difference whether you do right or wrong, a person's conscience ain't got no sense and just goes for him *anyway*. If I had a yaller dog that didn't know no more than a person's conscience does, I would pison him. It takes up more room than all the rest of a person's insides, and yet ain't no good, nohow. Tom Sawyer he says the same." Sorry, Huck, but no he don't. This genuine love and pity for humanity, which is how I read it, anyway, brings Huck closer to us than ever before, his vulnerability, his unflinching honesty, even if it hurts. He genuinely wants to set Jim free. The question now is how to do it?

In chapters thirty-four through thirty-eight, *Adventures of Huckleberry Finn* turns more into "The Tom Sawyer Show" as his goofy, Sir Walter Scott-influenced captured-prisoner demands on Jim reach ridiculous proportions. Huck takes a back seat here, and to many critics, this is where the novel falls short. As noted earlier, this is where Maria Konnikova's article is so interesting because she defends, on psychological grounds, how Huck behaves.

By the time we get to the end of chapter thirty-nine and Tom's "nonnamous" letters, we are ready for something to explode, and explode it does. The letters have, naturally, scared the pants off the Phelps' and a posse shows up with rifles, and after all the Tom-foolery (we can literally say that), we've gone through in the intervening chapters, it strikes home that, hey, this is serious. Somebody could get shot. Somebody could die. And while the fiddling and diddling in those previous four chapters does seem a bit much, the jolt when things do happen is unmistakable.

In what must have been a great release for him (reads that way, anyway), Twain steps on the accelerator, and after all that stultification and imprisonment, it becomes a Jason Bourne movie. As a reader, you're running right along with Jim and Huck as they're fired at while escaping the Phelps' plantation.

5. Navigating His Way to the Finish

The kids were breathless as we read this section. It's important make sure that when you get to this section, you have time to get through it. You see, Tom is wounded in the escape, and in a dramatic moment, realizes that he can't go on with Huck and Jim. Huck leaves him with Jim and goes off to get help. When help finally arrives, a wounded Tom is out of his head and the doctor, desperately, asks for help. Sure enough, one final time, out of the woods comes Jim, risking his freedom if not his life, to help the kid who had done nothing but torment and disrespect him. How John Wallace or Jane Smiley could read this scene and not understand Twain's intent, well, it's beyond me.

In the classroom, there were amazed looks everywhere. They had to talk about this.

What was Twain thinking, I asked them? Having a slave risk his freedom, coming out to help the doctor tend to Tom, who has done nothing but cause Jim trouble? Was he nuts? Would they do that for someone? My students said maybe, but not if he were white. "That's Twain's point, exactly," I said. The class was silent. "It was the right thing to do, wasn't it? Should color matter at that point?" "It shouldn't," said another student. "But it would." A third student agreed, saying, "But Jim is so good. And he's the adult, remember." There followed a lot more silence, a few nods. What would they do in such a situation? Hmmm ... nobody ever asked them that. It's a damn good thing to ask, isn't it? Over on the wall, I swear I saw a smile on the picture of Twain and his dog.

Twain has saved a few thunderbolts for the finish. Though wounded, Tom returns to the Phelps' place and lo and behold, Twain brings another character in: Tom's Aunt Polly shows up, and there's some comic relief as they play Who's on First for a bit. Amid the laughs, we also find out the *reason* Tom Sawyer didn't mind helping Huck free Jim, something that puzzled Huck for the longest time. Jim, Tom explains, was already free; Tom was just having fun with him. This got the kids. "He was free all the time?" asked one of them. "And they put him through all that?" Another student wrote that throughout the whole book, they thought it would end with Jim and Huck getting to the free slave states. This student also said that they didn't think Twain made a mistake, that it was entertaining the way Tom told the whole story, and that finding out Jim was free the whole time was really funny.

Huck also finds out, in the closing sentences, that the dead body he spotted in an old wrecked house they spotted on the river was Pap. "Well, den," Jim explains to Huck, "you k'n git yo money when you wants it; kase data wuz him." Huck, interestingly, offers no comment or reaction—but to change the subject. He leaves us, as you might expect, with a smile, and no doubt, at least some of the true sentiment of the author at finally completing this most troublesome manuscript. "Tom's most well, now," Huck writes in the closing paragraph,

> and got his bullet around his neck on a watchguard for a watch, and is always seeing what time it is, and so there ain't nothing more to write about, and I am rotten glad of it, because if I'd a knowed what a trouble it was to make a book I wouldn't a tackled it and ain't agoing to no more. But I reckon I got to light out for the Territory ahead of the rest, because aunt Sally, she's going to adopt me and sivilize me and I can't stand it. I been there before.
> The End, Yours Truly Huck Finn.

In a move that surely would have delighted Twain, the class broke into spontaneous applause at this point, and a couple of kids even stood, which I'm not sure how to read; are they happy they're done with the damn book or are they thrilled by its dramatic conclusion?

What I've found wonderful is that once you finish reading it—I always try to make sure we'll have some room to talk—they want to talk about it. It's not like some books that when you finish it, you're done. There's nothing else to say. *Huck Finn* isn't like that and maybe Twain wrote it that way.

While it is a bold thing to say, I've often seen something transformative in this book. That was the case, it seemed, for a student of mine, who said that when Huck reunited with an old pal, Tom Sawyer, his entire outlook on Jim changed. This student said this was the point that made people feel the ending was perhaps lacking, but agreed with Konnikova, who pointed out, "Twain wasn't taking an easy way out or wrapping up loose ends any which way he could. He was showing us ourselves as we actually are—as we change from the private (river) to the public (town) sphere, when of a sudden, others' eyes are on us. And that is not a pretty sight to behold." This student went on to say that it's nothing but the bare truth, and Twain's idea wasn't to make Huck a hero; he made him real. Huck is a thirteen-year-old; how'd you expect a preteen to act around a friend vs. an adult? Around their friends, they act like themselves, so Huck brought out his true colors, and that's what made the ending a true piece. I wouldn't argue with that because that was the most important lesson a person could learn. The people around you could make you or break you, but you have

5. Navigating His Way to the Finish

to decide for yourself on that situation, and ultimately, the decision you make is who you really are.

Another student went, I think, even deeper in their analysis. When I shared her comments with a veteran AP teacher from another state, she had to catch her breath. "My God, John," she said. "I got chillbumps." Me, too.

This student said that at first, she and the other students didn't see where the book would fit into their lives, as "nigger" was used 239 times in the book. She wrote that in a time when lynchings were the norm and slaves of the South were still thought to be 3/5th of a person, Twain spoke up.

This student observed that over a century later, his words still cause controversy, still shake the foundations of the land of the free, saying that was the hook and sinker for her. She said that knowing school districts in America did not want Huck to be taught unless 239 of its words were altered made it a no brainer … she knew she had to read it! In doing so, she saw herself in the adventure. She observed that there are hardships in everyone's life, but being from her community, the worst things were her normal, saying that if she had somewhere to run, she would … and that Huck and Jim ran for her. She wrote that she saw herself in them as they left their problems behind and ran for dear life. She saw the unbreakable bond built between them and noted that by reading it together, there was one built between her, her classmates, and myself.

This student ended her writing assignment by observing that while Huckleberry Finn had a duty to his country to turn in his running partner, Jim, he couldn't go against his conscience telling him he'd been taught wrong. His moral compass pulled him to Jim's side to help him get to his family, to freedom, and by doing so, Huck freed himself from the strong hold society had upon him. By telling this story, Twain hoped to free the people of his time from these chains as well. By reading this story, she observed, her and her classmates shackles—from whatever past each of them had, from the prejudice they had against any teacher which really wanted to teach us, from not knowing about a book which changed and is still changing America—fell once they read the last page.

6

A Critical Casserole—Who's Right?

With reading the novel complete, it's up to you how much further you'd like to go. I've found that the students really enjoy the ending and discussing it together. Usually the next day, I'll explain that many critics have suggested Twain ruins the ending by having Huck give way to Tom. Even Ernest Hemingway, after suggesting all American literature came from this book, dismissed the close of the book.

So also does Saunders, comically, in "The United States of Huck." In a section as direct as its title: "The Ending, Oh My God, the Ending," Saunders opens with a withering quote from critic Bernard DeVoto, another cutting paraphrase from Leo Marx, and then finally, Ernest's parting shot. Saunders says, "There is a kind of perverse greatness in the ending, in the sense that Waterloo was a great last battle for someone as considerable as Napoleon." As Saunders sees it, "Twain has written himself into a rough and very serious spot," he said. "Jim is being held prisoner in the Deep South by people used to holding prisoners..." People who would not have a problem killing a slave or severely punishing a white accomplice. For the book to be authentic, Twain's intent all along, how could the reader imagine Huck and Jim walking off into the sunset together? Author David Bradley, though, sees things a bit differently. As noted in a fine PBS guide,

> Writer David Bradley notes that many have criticized the ending of *Huck Finn* but "none of them has been able to suggest—much less write—a better ending.... They failed for the same reason that Twain wrote the ending as he did: America has never been able to write a better ending. America has never been able to write any ending at all." Or, it is something else. Writing in the October 2012 issue of Scientific American, author Maria Konnikova suggests that, psychologically speaking, there is nothing wrong with Huck's behavior. She explains it this way: "How could Huck, after building a friendship with

6. A Critical Casserole—Who's Right?

Jim for the duration of the book, after deepening his connection and realizing how much more there is to the man than the category "slave," just turn around and forget him like that? How can he fall back so easily into old habits, as if he hadn't grown at all from start to finish? It doesn't make sense.

I won't argue for or against the ending's artistic merits. That's a topic for another piece. But what I will say is that psychologically, Huck's about-face couldn't be more sound. Twain might have offended on other accounts, but there is one thing he got right: not only *could* Huck fall back to old ways at the tip of a hat—or the arrival of a Tom Sawyer, as the case may be—but he most likely *would* do so if he were a flesh-and-blood twelve year old fresh off a rafting adventure.

Brilliantly taking the age-old argument in a surprisingly sound scientific direction, she goes on to talk about peer pressure, their respective environments (the raft, Southern society) and, I think, she makes a lot of sense:

> In the same essay where he laments Huck's fall from heroic grace to Tom Sawyer's old sidekick, (Leo) Marx comments on Jim's problematic decline as well: "It should be added at once that Jim doesn't mind [the change in Huck] too much. The fact is that he has undergone a similar transformation. On the raft he was an individual, man enough to denounce Huck when Huck made him the victim of a practical joke. In the closing episode, however, we lose sight of Jim in the maze of farcical invention. On the raft, Jim was in a new environment, where old rules need not apply—especially given its private nature. But how quickly old ways kick back in, irrespective of whether you were a Huck or a Jim in that prior context.

Reading this essay with my class gave us a chance to talk about environments and behavior. For example, in a school setting, how students react to a teacher may be very different than if they ran into that teacher in the mall. Not to mention how they might behave if they were with a bunch of kids, or by themselves. They connected with this, in a big way. Not only that, but Konnikova also addresses Jane Smiley's criticisms:

> Smiley takes her criticism on this point a step further. There is a chasm between Huck's stated affection for Jim and his willingness to then act on it, especially in these final episodes. She blames the divide on Twain's racism. *But wouldn't it be more correct to blame Huck's only too real humanity? It's that same break between the private and the public, the new and the habitual. All too often, there is a disconnect between feeling, what we say, and action, what we do about it* [Italics mine].

Considering that discussion and all that has built up to it, tell me *Huck Finn* isn't current. Go ahead.

Teaching *Huckleberry Finn*

So current, in fact, that reading novelist Jayne Ann Phillips' afterword in our Signet Classics paperback edition of *Huck Finn*, we may see the entire ending as prescient, considering the present political situation. That's if you extend her ideas just a little bit. She wrote it in 2008. Acknowledging decades of critical upheaval, Phillips demurs as she closes her Afterword:

> Critics from Hemingway to Doctorow have questioned the resolution of Huckleberry Finn, when Tom Sawyer appears and takes charge of the plot, as a failure of nerve or inspiration. Not so, Reader. Here the novel comes full circle, still bitterly "funny" more and more savage, into Twain's own "heart of darkness." The charming Tom "respectable and well brung up, and had a character to lose," becomes "Mars Tom" who manipulates Jim and co-opts Huck for his own entertainment, then pays Jim forty dollars for his time. Jim has saved his life, no matter. Tom Sawyer, friend and coconspirator, innocent as a mint julep or magnolia blossom, is evil come to life, unforgivable, unredeemable, unto the next generation.

In a comment that echoes the darkness that would inhabit Twain's end-of-civilization work, *A Connecticut Yankee In King Arthur's Court*, which he would write some four years later, Phillips convincingly sums it up this way: "Tom Sawyer, beloved representative of American boyhood, becomes in Twain's deliberate inversion, the dark reprobate, the true representative of horror, a blond Kurtz recovering in a feather bed, tended by the good aunts Sally and Polly." As I read that now, several years after she wrote it, Tom is a character who says the right things, pushes buttons that only he seems to sense, convinces everyone that he and he alone can fix what seems to be an insoluble problem, and to just trust him. Hmmmm. Can he can make America great again?

Though George Saunders wrote his Introduction long before anyone would have mentioned a character like Donald Trump would be running for president, the issues Saunders talks about in the closing section of "The United States of Huck," seem remarkably on-the-money. As Saunders goes on to explain about the two sides of the American nature, something has a familiar ring. "Tom likes kings, codified nobility, unquestioned privilege," he writes. Or, perhaps to update it, "Tom (Don) likes being worshipped, lots of attention, being able to write (tweet) exactly what he feels like saying, regardless of who he might upset or offend." Earlier, Saunders explains: "The United States of Tom looks at misery and says: Hey, I didn't do it. It looks at inequity and says: All my life, I've busted my butt to get

6. A Critical Casserole—Who's Right?

where I am, don't come crying to me." As far as I know, this was written long before Donald Trump's campaign platform was created, but whatever your political persuasion, doesn't this sentiment sound stunningly familiar?

Is there something in the character of Tom Sawyer, a fast-thinking, sweet-talking con man that is elemental to America? Think of how many times "the con" is part of Twain's story, people misrepresenting who they really are: Tom as Sarah Williams, the king and the duke as, well, the king and duke, Huck as Tom, Tom as Sid. Samuel Clemens as Mark Twain.

Could it be that Huck, the sweet, compassionate, mostly unlettered but whip-smart ugly duckling with a heart of gold is who we all wish we could be? Do we wish we could open our hearts the way Huck does and really, in perhaps Twain's bravest achievement in this novel, the way Jim does?

Again, this scene may well be what Twain was aiming for all along, the moral point of the novel in a nutshell. Huck, Jim and Tom have finally escaped from the Phelps' plantation, and in the commotion Tom Sawyer gets shot in the leg. Huck has gone for help, and Jim, now free, is hiding. And one last time, Twain conjures up a test of character for his black character, one more over the top test for him to show Tom (and really, white America—that's who he's writing for, after all) that humanity transcends race, that it is now and always should be about people, not color. And Twain pulls it off.

Justifiably, Huck's dramatic moment in chapter thirty-one, where he decides between Hell or not, gets most of the critical attention. It stops the show and is designed to. But this closing test for Jim, this one last showcase, is vital to appreciating the novel, to my way of thinking.

Imagine, for a moment, you're Jim. Finally, after what seems (and reads) like an endless struggle to gain your freedom, you're just steps away from a new life and you see this young white kid who's been sort of good-naturedly tormenting you for weeks now about to succumb to a gunshot wound and you see a struggling doctor about to lose him and ... you know, you know you just must help. And so you do. You come to help ... knowing that you're very likely sacrificing your personal freedom, and maybe your life, for someone else. Do we have people like that in our country right now? I hope so. I'd like to think so. But I wonder if they're still in the woods, waiting.

I've taught *Huck* for a while now, and it still surprises me how relevant it continues to be. There is something beneath the surface in the relationship between Huck and Jim: a kid who's seen way more than is recommended for someone his age and Jim, a husband and dad who simply could no longer endure his life as a slave and had to take drastic measures—as Huck did.

Though it is unspoken and remains so throughout the twists and turns of the book, maybe their mutual quest for freedom, and an inner sense that there *has* to be more to life than this, drove them to these extremes. As we read it, Twain has kept the narrative so swiftly moving—like the Mississippi—that we don't see these moves as extreme as they truly are. Huck clearly needs to get the heck out of there and the only way he can think of to put an end to the nonsense with Pap is to pretend he's dead. Of course, that's not something any of us would ever do, but we go along with it and believe that Huck is clever enough and desperate enough to pull it off.

In the classroom, this was perhaps the first moment where Huck's unschooled intelligence and his quick thinking seemed to catch the students' attention. It was as if they were thinking, "Yeah, I could do that. Cool." From their viewpoint, Jim's desperation was even more real and relatable. As we read about Jim describing his escape and how he had to run away, I looked out across the classroom at all their faces, imagining what it must be like for them to read about the struggles of this good man, a representation of one of their ancestors. What would it be like to grow up and not have a choice? That may be, in a nutshell, one reason why teaching at a school like mine is such a challenge because who would want to teach a bunch of kids who knew there was no way out, who had trouble caring about school, who were mostly there because society and the law said they had to be? Truthfully, there are students we have like that every year. Our goal, of course, is to show them that there are ways out. Like Jim, they can escape.

It must not have been easy for Twain to imagine how a slave might think and speak in a realistic way when he was confronted with the realities of 1840s America. While there are moments when Twain reverts to a portrait of Jim where he seems more like someone who wandered off the stage of a minstrel show, there are other remarkably tender, insightful, touching scenes where we see and feel the soul of a great man.

Though Twain was one of the most well-known religious skeptics of his or any time, religion comes up often enough and is treated respectfully

6. A Critical Casserole—Who's Right?

enough for us to wonder, as Huck did, does it work? Why *are* we here? Was Huck put on Earth to free Jim or was he to serve as part of His (or Her) plan to demonstrate to the world that a white kid and a black man can be best friends, can trust and rely on each other?

Certainly, there will be some who think a discussion at this level is way beyond the comprehension of high school students. There are those who will further argue that liberal arts, and students who might not be headed for college spending time reading a classic book, is a waste. "Teach him or her a trade," they say. "Show them how to fill out a tax return. Do something practical. They don't need to know Twain or Shakespeare." How can inexperienced readers intelligently discuss the ending of a major American novel? What do they know about it, anyway? What is the point?

These are good questions, I suppose. It is impossible to truly measure what sort of impact this or any novel has on anyone. Am I a better person, a more thoughtful teacher and compassionate adult because I read Twain and other great writers growing up? I would say yes, but could I prove it? Do I need to take a standardized test and score well to prove it? As I hope is evident by the depth of the many and varied discussions in this book, closely reading Twain or any other great writer enriches you and your students in ways that are difficult to measure but un-debatable.

And, as we begin to discuss the ending and the controversy surrounding it, you wonder, did Twain write the book for literary critics or for the masses? When you're reading a book that has lasted the way *Huck* has, you can't help but think why. You also can't help but wonder if the critics don't have a point, considering so many of them seem to agree on Twain's rocky ending.

But helping your students to evaluate this novel the same way they would a film or TV show or anything else is important, I think. It's critical thinking. Don't we all need that? If, by the end of the book, they have some ideas on what *should* happen and the author doesn't lead them there, they want to know why. And they should want to know why. Until you've been in a classroom and seen and felt the impact of a story, a poem, a film, a song or something that connects with the students in a way that most things don't, it may be difficult to see and measure the benefit. Isn't that one of the issues we face as educators now? How do we measure the gains these kids have made over the course of a year? As Twain allegedly said, "I never let schooling interfere with my education."

Teaching *Huckleberry Finn*

If you read the depth in their writing or listen to the thoughtful discussion of a class after they've completed *Huck Finn*, there is simply no question that they learned something and probably had a memorable experience with the novel. If they cannot demonstrate that on a test or a quiz, does that mean it didn't happen? In a numbers-driven society, it's natural, I suppose to want to have some simple way to prove that Charlie is smarter today than he was when he first took the class. But as we know, the way literature works is much more difficult to measure.

To give a literary example, Joseph Heller's *Catch 22* is a carefully crafted cyclical novel that leads the reader through a series of events and a wide range of characters who, gradually, as the story unfolds, reveal more and more information with each successive chapter. This was the author's intent, as he wanted all the revelations to occur in simultaneous fashion—that was what he was going for. I knew someone who, instead of following's Heller's construction, went through all the chapters named "Yossarian," then all the ones with "Major Danby" and so on until they had all the plot lines and events down. What they did not have was the same understanding of the entirety of the novel, how all those events fit together. On a who-did-what sort of test, the student would excel. On the overall impact and grasp and significance of the novel, good luck.

To me, *Huckleberry Finn* is such a rich book to study. There can be lasting importance to what Twain is writing about. I used it as my first novel in teaching an advanced placement class on English language and composition this past year. The overarching goal was to prepare students for this slam-bang, four-hour Mount Everest–like test at the end of the school year. While overall the track record wasn't good—only 44 percent of the students who took the test across the nation passed—there were signs of excellence in there if you knew where to look. One of my students ranked among the top 25 percent of students across America in one very difficult multiple-choice category. Another two of my students ranked among the top 25 in rhetorical analysis. And so on. Overall, five students or two more than I could have predicted before the test began, came very close to passing. To my way of thinking, the complexities of *Huckleberry Finn* helped them prepare for that challenge.

So, I say go as deep as you can. If you want your students to grasp the idea of an author's purpose, well, put them in Twain's shoes. How does he end his novel? How do the characters act at the end of the work, and is it what you'd expect? By this time, your students know Huck. They know

6. A Critical Casserole—Who's Right?

Jim. They know the environment the two find themselves in. They have their own opinions. What is literary criticism but someone else's opinion? That many suggest the novel is flawed, particularly the ending, is also undeniable. But this is also undeniable: what other author of that era even dared attempt what Twain did? Did anyone else take what clearly seems to be a stand on behalf of African-Americans?

To me, this seems to be something often lost in the process of evaluating something written so long ago, namely, the context. You can argue, and some do, that a work of art should stand alone, that you don't need to know when or why or how it was written. That was one of the arguments for Common Core, where to some educators, there should be no backstory given to the students; they should be able to discern it from the work alone. "Take two weeks on Lincoln's Gettysburg Address" one video urged. "Let the work shine through." Hmmm. 10 classroom days for 272 words. Try and see how your kids will act doing the same 272-word speech for two weeks. These things are not written in a vacuum, there are reasons and responses and reactions and they can be very important.

That's why when some critics, Leo Marx, for instance, criticize Twain for "having a lack of nerve" to finish *Huck Finn* the way Leo thinks he should, it doesn't ring true. Shouldn't it matter that Twain was the first American writer to create a more three-dimensional black character than had been seen before?

Which brings us back to Jane Smiley, whom we mentioned earlier in the book. One of the unusual things about American literature, it seems, is that every so often in the life of a novel, some big shot, whether it's T.S. Eliot or D.H. Lawrence or a somebody re-reading *Moby Dick* 40 years after it came out, there seems to be this great re-evaluation or a major reconsideration of the original work. Even though not a word has changed in the interim. This is somewhat like a retired major-league baseball player being denied entrance to the Hall of Fame for 15 years, then suddenly appearing at the top of the ballot and getting in. It wasn't like he did anything to improve his record; sometimes, it takes a while to sort things out.

This seems to be what Smiley, an accomplished and well-respected novelist, was going for in 1996 when she offered a new assessment of Twain's classic called "Say It Ain't So, Huck," written for Harper's Magazine, she explains, after she'd fallen and broken her leg (I'm not making this up). It seems that when Smiley was recovering from her broken leg, she thought it would be time to re-read a childhood classic, *Huckleberry*

Teaching *Huckleberry Finn*

Finn. She was displeased with what she found this time around: "...I closed the cover stunned," she writes. "Yes, stunned. Not, by any means, by the artistry of the book but by the notion that this is the novel that all American literature grows out of, that this is a great novel, that this is even a serious novel." You don't even think *Huck* is a serious novel? Explain yourself: "Although Huck had his fans at publication, his real elevation into the pantheon was worked out early in the Propaganda Era, between 1948 and 1955, by Lionel Trilling, Leslie Fiedler, T. S. Eliot, Joseph Wood Krutch, and some lesser lights, in the introductions to American and British editions of the novel and in such journals as *Partisan Review* and *The New York Times Book Review*." The Propaganda Era, huh? Hmmm.

To Smiley, the reasons for the ascension of the book, she writes, were clear: "The requirements of Huck's installation rapidly revealed themselves: the failure of the last twelve chapters (in which Huck finds Jim imprisoned on the Phelps plantation and Tom Sawyer is reintroduced and elaborates a cruel and unnecessary scheme for Jim's liberation) had to be diminished, accounted for, or forgiven; after that, the novel's special qualities had to be placed in the context first of other American novels (to their detriment) and then of world literature." Why would such seemingly sharp, respected critics be hoodwinked about the novel? Smiley thinks it was his style—and T.S. Eliot:

> The best bets here seemed to be Twain's style and the river setting, and the critics invested accordingly: Eliot, who had never read the novel as a boy, traded on his own childhood beside the big river, elevating Huck to the Boy, and the Mississippi to the River God, therein finding the sort of mythic resonance that he admired. Trilling liked the river god idea, too, though he didn't bother to capitalize it. He also thought that Twain, through Huck's lying, told truths, one of them being (I kid you not) that "something ... had gone out of American life after the [Civil War], some simplicity, some innocence, some peace."

Looking back at this bit of criticism in 2017 does seem a bit silly. But when it was written, when we consider the context of Trilling's comment, it may not have been silly at all. Interestingly, when Norman Mailer accepted an assignment from the New York Times to write an appreciation of *Huck* for the 100th anniversary of its publication, he began by quoting old, dead-wrong book reviews.

Smiley, swinging for the critical fences here, says, "But, in fact, *The Adventures of Huckleberry Finn* has little to offer in the way of greatness.

6. A Critical Casserole—Who's Right?

There is more to be learned about the American character *from* its canonization than *through* its canonization." As if sensing an audible gasp from readers across America, she tried to soften the baseball bat to the kneecap with her next paragraph: "Let me hasten to point out that, like most others, I don't hold any grudges against Huck himself. He's just a boy trying to survive. The villain here is Mark Twain, who knew how to give Huck a voice but didn't know how to give him a novel." Take that, Mr. Twain. To Smiley, where Twain first went wrong was he strayed too far from home:

> Four hundred pages into it, having just passed Cairo and exhausted most of his memories of Hannibal and the upper Mississippi, Twain put the manuscript aside for three years. He was facing a problem every novelist is familiar with: his original conception was beginning to conflict with the implications of the actual story. It is at this point in the story that Huck and Jim realize two things: they have become close friends, and they have missed the Ohio River and drifted into what for Jim must be the most frightening territory of all–down the river, the very place Miss Watson was going to sell him to begin with. Jim's putative savior, Huck, has led him as far astray as a slave can go, and the farther they go, the worse it is going to be for him. Because the Ohio was not Twain's territory, the fulfillment of Jim's wish would necessarily lead the novel away from the artistic integrity that Twain certainly sensed his first four hundred pages possessed. He found himself writing not a boy's novel, like *Tom Sawyer*, but a man's novel, about real moral dilemmas and growth.

Which, I would say, is exactly what Twain *was* doing, setting up real moral dilemmas and personal growth challenges for Huck and Jim and delivering on them throughout the rest of the novel—though I grant that there were some sticky moments with the ending.

To Smiley, that was because of how Twain truly felt about his characters from the start: "As with all bad endings, the problem really lies at the beginning, and at the beginning of *The Adventures of Huckleberry Finn* neither Huck nor Twain takes Jim's desire for freedom at all seriously; that is, they do not accord it the respect that a man's passion deserves." Huh? To Smiley, Twain should have had them cross the Mississippi, land in Illinois and be done with it.

As Roy Blount, Jr., said in a delightful *Huckleberry Finn* panel held in New York City (available on Youtube) sometime after Smiley's criticisms, "Dawn Powell once said that criticisms of her latest novel boiled down to the critics saying that if they had my automobile, they wouldn't go visit my folks, they'd go visit theirs." Later in the same program, authors William

Teaching *Huckleberry Finn*

Styron and Shelby Foote argue against Ms. Smiley's offering of a novel to study from that era—Harriet Beecher Stowe's *Uncle Tom's Cabin*, which she claims is the real deal, instead of *Huckleberry Finn*. "My own feeling about Jane Smiley, a novelist of extreme intelligence," Styron says,

> is that this is one of the stupidest essays ever written. I read it with growing dread and fascination as I realized there was some sort of ghastly subtext there which I couldn't quite grasp but that every other sentence was either a canard or an exaggeration or to my mind, an outright lie.
>
> I think the place where she misses the point most directly and most stupidly, is, and I'm going to quote it, "To give credit to Huck suggests the only racial insight Americans of the 19th and 20th century are capable of is a recognition of the obvious, that blacks, slave and free, are human. Now on the surface that's perfectly unexceptional until you examine it in the light of Huck Finn himself. Because to my mind, the vivid moral courage of Huck Finn himself the boy, the 12-year-old boy, is that he's the only person in the book, virtually the only white person, that does see Jim is human. This is a time, a slave period of unspeakable horror and cruelty in which black people were bought and sold routinely, like animals. And I think when you examine the character of Huck Finn, you see that he's the only one who recognizes Jim's humanity.

"I make it practically valueless," historian and novelist Shelby Foote said of Smiley's article for Harpers. "I judge a novel in large part by its writing. I think as a novelist, I know a great novel from a bad novel. *Huckleberry Finn* is a great novel and *Uncle Tom's Cabin* is a bad novel. Now I can't back that up, I just believe it. That's my sense of reading the two books. I've never finished *Uncle Tom's Cabin*."

Author Justin Kaplan, a Twain historian, aimed his comments at my audience, high school kids: "I can imagine a young black high school student in a teaching situation in a high school being horribly mortified or hurt by the 231 uses of the word 'nigger'—and by the way, you'll find not quite so many uses of the word in *Uncle Tom's Cabin* and no one squawks about that. But it does cause pain. And the way to answer that is *Huckleberry Finn* is not *Little House on the Prairie* and one of the functions of great fiction is to disorient and dismay and to upset and make you think differently. And this book certainly does it."

Styron may have had the closing word on Twain: "It's amazing to me that he had so little racism," Styron said, "given the fact that he was a child of his time, that he grew up in a town that had slavery and that he joined briefly, the Confederate Army, I'm astounded that this book with this

6. A Critical Casserole—Who's Right?

heavy weight of race consciousness and the heavy burden of hatred that hung over Missouri at the time, that the book is so free of these horrible things for so many years."

According to the Third Norton Critical Edition, more than 11 million students over 50 years have read Twain's classic. Sorry, but that kicks *Uncle Tom's Cabin* in the seat of his pants. As it should.

A while back, before starting on this book, I wrote to Hal Holbrook, who happened to be bringing his one-man Mark Twain Tonight show a few hours away from me. I shared my experiences with the novel in my classroom and wanted to hear his response: "I'm really happy to hear about the reaction you get to *Huckleberry Finn* in your classroom and that it comes from black and mostly poor students," Holbrook wrote. "That's very encouraging. I've often wondered if you just let young people read the book and not preach to them about, do they get it? I find it hard to believe that young black kids today will not be offended by the use of the word "nigger" if the reasons for using it are not explained to them. He doesn't use the word that much in *Tom Sawyer* or *Pudd'n'head Wilson*. In *Huck*, he was using it as a sledge hammer of embarrassment."

Holbrook, of course, has continued to perform his *Mark Twain Tonight* one-man show across America. There is a DVD available of an entire show, one that appeared on network television in 1967. It's in color, is very well-done, and apparently so well done that Holbrook has let that stand as a representative of the show. There has been several vinyl albums released of additional onstage material over the years but never a second DVD or video release. Having had a chance to see Holbrook's performance on four separate occasions through the years, he could certainly have done Volume II with entirely different material. He has more than 20 hours of Twain material committed to memory. From all accounts, a wonderful documentary film directed by Scott Teems, *Twain/Holbrook: An American Odyssey*, which captures Holbrook's recent shows, made the documentary festival circuit in 2014 to rave reviews but is currently unavailable. There are trailer clips available on Youtube.

Happily, when it came to my classroom, I think the kids understood the novel as I think Twain intended. There is a genuine sense of momentum as we come down to the finish line. The book's dramatic final chapters, where Tom is wounded during the exciting escape, Jim's one last act of heroism almost always has students engaged and excited.

And when Tom finally lets slip that Jim is actually free, that Miss

Teaching *Huckleberry Finn*

Watson had freed him in her will, well, there's almost always an eruption of students, some exclaiming about Jim went through everything he did not knowing he was free, and others remarking on how Twain set up this plot point, with one student remarking that it was almost as if Twain knew readers would be stunned by the news.

When it came to writing about the novel, their pens were on fire. One student wrote that *Huckleberry Finn* put a twist in their life because it used the "N" word too freely, and that they were upset before they understood the full meaning and message behind the story. However, as this student continued reading, they remembered Ernest Hemingway's quote: "There was nothing before. There's been nothing as good since." To this student, Hemingway's quote is understandable because if you pay attention, the book starts off a little on the edge by using the "n" word too freely, but once you get down to the nitty gritty, you've never experienced great literature until you've dived inside *Huckleberry Finn*.

Another student agreed, saying that *Huckleberry Finn* was one of the most honest books they'd ever read. She said it gave so much life, truth and a certain rawness that you couldn't turn your head away from the book. She went on to say that you can't find a pure book like this nowadays. A third student said that she'd never been so interested in a book, and that Twain took on the debates of his day (and could represent ours) and made it real. She said that for Twain to create such a masterpiece changed the game.

Yet another student had a nice take on everything. She said that Twain took the risk to write about something that was unacceptable back then and took the chance to write about a topic that everyone else was scared to even mention. She said this reminded her of Thoreau, who she called a writer who was not scared to talk or write about anything. This student continued by saying that in her eyes, the purpose of *Huckleberry Finn* was to mention events that happened in the past, particularly how people of color were treated, and that it's a way to remember something important and see how things have changed for the better.

This student closed her essay with a lovely and appropriate quote from the novel to make her teacher proud: "That is just the way of some people," she wrote, quoting chapter one. "They get down on a thing when they don't know nothing about it." Nice. That's an exact quote from Mark Twain, writing in the opening chapter of his greatest work, *The Adventures of Huckleberry Finn*.

7

Incorrect Correctness, Another Flawed Finish

The bulk of this book was written and about ready to submit to the publisher when the 2016–2017 school year began. Since I'd had a chance to teach *Huck* for several years already, it seemed like an appropriate time to send it in. Then, the day before school was to begin, I was asked to teach advanced placement language and composition—an AP course. Cool. Something I'd been angling for and something our struggling school hadn't dared offer in many years.

Considering my previous success with the novel, I planned to begin the year with *Huckleberry Finn*. With its literary complexity, its humor, and overall significance in the history of literature, I thought it was perfect; what a way to start a year! Our principal was on board, as I'd had considerable success with the novel in the previous years, so hey, let's go. I submitted my syllabus to her and to the College Board, which must sign off on your syllabus for your course to be accredited. I figured I was all set to go.

I began teaching the novel with my usual enthusiasm and, as always, it took a bit for the students to get into it. But while we were working on it, there was a catch, a catch I just didn't think about. Since it had been so long since our school had attempted an AP course, the three East Gadsden High administrators the College Board had on their books were not only no longer at the school, we weren't sure where they were.

Since our principal had so many other things on her plate, she was happy to hand off the AP syllabus issue to two of her assistant principals, something I came to suspect they had been laying for all along. Why do I say that? You see, the principal had already approved syllabus one, but she was not the administrator listed by the College Board. They needed new names. Now if these administrators wanted to keep my original, already approved syllabus, all these administrators had to do was rubber-stamp it and send it in to the College Board.

When they did not do that and went to the trouble of calling the College Board to tell them changes were forthcoming, then didn't talk to me or reply to my emails for a few weeks, I knew something was up. In talking with other AP teachers, this was not standard procedure. Administrators generally don't construct syllabi, particularly for a course neither one of them were qualified to teach. At the time, I didn't understand the significance of this. Since I was knee-deep in trying to wrangle a class of 25 kids into high-level reading and writing, I let it go for a few weeks while I built my course. And we began reading *Huckleberry Finn*.

We were about 15 chapters in and the class was really starting to connect with the novel. This is when Huck and Jim are separated for the first time as a nasty fog comes over the Mississippi, foreshadowing a more permanent separation in a chapter or two. For a few moments, the class was concerned. What will happen to the two characters, lost out on the river, especially the runaway slave, their ancestor? All was quiet. We were reading it together every day. It's intense, dramatic. Everyone was all in.

Then one morning, we were at a key moment in the novel. After a desperate and dramatic search, Huck finally tracks down the battered, leaf-strewn raft, their raft, and finds a worn-out Jim asleep. Even though they'd gotten along and were truly growing close, Huck decides to try and embarrass Jim for some reason, and whether it's childishness or meanness, we're not sure. This is always a pivotal moment when we're reading the book, for once Jim woke up and saw Huck he was thrilled and thankful his friend was back. Somewhat coldly, Huck claimed that the unlettered slave had just dreamed all their trouble with the storm, that the separation of the two of them was just a mirage, a dream. Huck tries to convince Jim that Huck has been on the raft the whole time. As he did, the class grew a bit uneasy. They knew what Huck was trying to pull. Jim's just a slave. He can't fight back, not really. Can he? Not against white folk.

"Keep in mind," I said to the class, just as an assistant principal somewhat unexpectedly entered my classroom and took a seat at the back, "this is a teenager saying this to a grown man. A black man who has, to this point, looked out for him as no other adult male has. Yet Huck embarrasses him. So badly that for perhaps the first time in American literature, Jim, a black man, ends up telling Huck off." A mild cheer from the class. The assistant principal takes a note.

7. Incorrect Correctness, Another Flawed Finish

Then I read Huck's apology aloud. "It was fifteen minutes," I read to the silent class, "before I could work myself up to go and humble myself to a nigger—but I done it, and I warn't ever sorry for it afterwards, neither." The girl in front of me swallowed hard. "Imagine someone from Alabama or Mississippi," I said to the class, "or some place still very bitter about the defeat in the Civil War reading that, wondering if maybe someday they too would have to apologize to a, well..." It was then the assistant principal got up and stormed out of my classroom. Would "stormed" be too strong a word? A few minutes later, after the bell, she was waiting outside my classroom. There would be a meeting with me and her and another assistant principal immediately after school.

I had barely sat down in the tiny office of one when the other erupted: "*Huckleberry Finn*? Oh, my god, I cannot believe you are teaching *this* book? In *our school*?" she said. "Oh my God! I have never read this book, would never *read* this book and I can't *believe* you are teaching it in our school in this day and age!" That was our new assistant principal. She'd never actually *read* the book, but she *knew* of it. Oh. "Why," she continued, "aren't you teaching *Their Eyes Were Watching God* or *Beloved* or *To Kill a Mockingbird*?" What she wanted to know was why, while teaching black kids in a black school, I wasn't sticking with *black* books. Why not teach books that just about every single other teacher at our school and just about teacher at every other black school uses?

Well, if you've read this far, you know why I didn't choose those books. I'm not teaching black kids, I'm teaching kids who happen to be black or Hispanic. To my mind, they didn't need to be shielded from anything. While Twain's book is controversial, especially to those who haven't read it, wouldn't it be smarter to examine and explain some of the difficult things that these kids were sure to experience in life, with a teacher they respected and trusted, than to let them out into the world thinking that everybody thinks like Atticus Finch (or, anyway, the Atticus Finch of *To Kill a Mockingbird*)? Isn't that education? And the ultimate point of the book is that regardless of race, if two people respect each other, they can be friends. Great friends. Like Huck and Jim, despite what society says.

Without reading the book, of course, these administrators would know none of this. They knew about a word. A word that may be in, what, three out of five rap songs that these kids listen to? A word they hear in the hallways and the lunchroom and on the bus? A word that, sadly, pulls down a shade over a window of understanding? Why am I sharing this?

Teaching *Huckleberry Finn*

Because this scenario or something like this either already has happened or will in administrators' offices across our country. Earlier in the year, these administrators talked about the students as "customers." "We have to think about pleasing the customers," one said.

It was interesting to me that in the meeting when they spoke of the students, it was always "the children, the children." Children? These were 11th and 12th graders, many of whom had very adult responsibilities. Three students in that graduating class had children and two others had to miss the last weeks of school because they were in the hospital delivering their babies. The last thing they needed was for someone to filter life for them.

A few weeks after I had pulled the book, I went to speak to the principal, who, she said, had not been informed about the administrators' plan or their meeting. When she asked me what reason they gave for the meeting, I told her what they told me: "The administrators said a couple of the kids had said they were uncomfortable," I said. Her answer was worthy and thoughtful and perfect and I wish every principal in America could echo it in moments like this: "So?"

And she went on to say what every teacher and administrator should already know, that there's value in a students learning to deal with uncomfortable feelings and situations, that life will not come at them in "comfortable" waves, and that that's part of learning, teaching, growing, and maturing. Unfortunately, her sensible answer came too late to save the day.

Sadly, it seems as if this political auto-correct, this overprotective mania is sweeping through schools across the country. There seems to be so many ways to offend someone these days that many schools, I fear, will hesitate to teach a difficult, challenging novel like *Huckleberry Finn* and opt for something safer. Are we that afraid of upsetting our students and their parents? I think sometimes, the answer is yes! Don't they trust that we're teaching material that they will need? Not sure about that one.

Teaching class the next day after that "meeting" was difficult. On the ride home and all throughout that evening, I was angry, first. How could someone who hadn't even read *Huckleberry Finn* be so willing to condemn it? How could someone so clearly uninformed be making decisions on what anybody was doing in their classroom? They did not insist that I stop the novel, but did they have to? I could see where this was headed. How could I continue to teach the novel the way it deserved with this kind of administrative neck squeezing?

7. Incorrect Correctness, Another Flawed Finish

I pulled it. I walked into the classroom, told the students that this was where Twain put the novel aside for several years and so were we. There were no protests, no groans or heavy sighs. I explained that if they wanted to read ahead, they could hang onto their books for a few weeks. A handful did. At the end of the year, several mentioned how much reading Huck, well, about half of it, had meant to them. We hadn't even gotten to chapter thirty-one yet.

Over the course of the summer, I had a chance to attend an AP literature seminar in Atlanta and shared my plans for the book and a few stories about the year. I shared a few excerpts from this book with Hepsibah Roskelly, one of the College Board's most respected lecturers, who taught the Atlanta seminar. When I shared some of what I had written, she recognized right away what was going on and what I was trying to do. I asked her to share her thoughts with my readers: "You understand so well the controversy Huck continues to represent," she wrote. "It's true that the book doesn't so much *provoke* controversy as it exposes it. To me, that's the problem with it, the reason your ill-prepared and reactionary asst. principal was so horrified at your teaching the book with the terrible word: it lays bare just how little, and how poorly, we've grappled with race in this country. After she'd read about the "mugging," she was sympathetic:

> [That meeting] was a sad reminder of how we continue to evade race and racism. Particularly sad since so few books have done what Twain does, demonstrate how people can actually learn to be human. Huck comes to see Jim as human and that makes Huck himself human. I like so much all the discussion you give of critics who decry Huck's turn away from Jim when Tom comes on the scene. Being human is never a done deal, is it? We have to learn it again and again and most painfully when we have to challenge those we have admired or have owed something to [best friends, parents, teachers, institutions...]

Roskelly continued:

> Interestingly, you mention Atticus Finch as an "easier" sell to administrators who want to avoid the difficulties of race. That book is not as easy as some would have it, of course, and reading the sequel, which puts Atticus in something of the quandary Huck faces with the return of Tom, suggests how very difficult it is to disown race prejudice once and for all. I am moved by your noble efforts to teach your students how to read with understanding, nuance and the power that comes from feeling the spark of connection. Whatever happens, know that you can harness that energy to use in whatever books you decide to teach. And someday you will teach Huck again. There's a reason that our Huck persists, despite the continual attempts to discredit and disown him.

Teaching *Huckleberry Finn*

As someone who speaks to high school educators from coast to coast, Roskelly's view of the situation in America is frightening: "You know that your problem is a problem nationwide in school systems because race is a nationwide issue," she wrote, "because a lack of reading skill and a refusal to read with imagination and insight is a nationwide problem. (Maybe especially among school administrators!) But I hope it gives you some comfort and help in knowing that one other teacher admires and understands what you're accomplishing with the young American scholars you teach."

Of course, I was touched by her kind letter and appreciate the opportunity to share it. Coming from someone with her experience and expertise, she's deeply concerned about where we are headed. The idea of teaching is to challenge, to open the minds of our students, and not close them.

While that administrator has moved on from the school, the attitude has remained. When asked about the summer seminar and my plans for this year and possibly a new course, AP literature, I mentioned that the two works recommended to everyone were *Hamlet* and *Huckleberry Finn*, because of their complexity and timeless quality. "*Hamlet* is fine," one said. "The other one, let's not even discuss it."

So, my classroom set of Twain's classic novel is jammed into a cabinet in the corner. Interrupted in mid-journey, their spines bent and roughed up, corners of the pages bent back, unread pages wondering why they were banished to the darkness of the closet again, I bet there was some grumbling. If you came in at just the right time, I bet you could smell a corncob pipe, maybe hear some cussin' and sort of a low chuckle. Banned again.

Looking back, I think the decision to teach the novel was a good one. For the past seven years—once my students got used to hearing him use the "N" word in sharing his story—Huck has been a most welcome visitor in my classroom. Truthfully, it's been one of the thrills of my teaching career to see these students who don't consider themselves readers annually get themselves caught up in Twain's tale, dipping their toes in the Ol' Muddy for 50 minutes every day. Homework doesn't happen. We read the whole thing—in class.

Something about Twain's brave and funny message of racial harmony, the way the strength and beauty and humanity in Huck and Jim's relationship unfolds with all its rifts and snags, grabs them in a way that most other novels don't.

7. Incorrect Correctness, Another Flawed Finish

Maybe I am too naive. Too idealistic for my own good. To me, it seems wrong to think our black students will never know a white person, never work with a white person, will always and forever hold the scar of slavery across their heart, clogging the arteries that flow to their brain so completely that no book, no matter how beautiful, how heart-rending; no matter how sincerely Twain tries to show America how ugly it truly was in his own lifetime, risking his reputation, popularity, and career simply because it was the right thing to do; that none of that will now or ever matter to them or anyone else. Sure, it's easy to dismiss it before even trying to understand or finding out for yourself. There are annual protests over *Huck* ever since I can remember. There probably always will be. Does that mean you shouldn't teach it?

Noted African-American author Toni Morrison warned us about this sort of thing some years ago when she wrote an introduction titled "This Amazing, Troubling Book," for another new edition of *Huckleberry Finn*. Her own understanding of the book, she said, had changed over time. Twain's work was more carefully crafted, more deliberate than she originally thought: "The withholdings at critical moments, which I once took to be deliberate evasions, stumbles even, or a writer's impatience with his or her material, I began to see as otherwise: as entrances, crevices, gaps, seductive invitations flashing the possibility of meaning," Morrison wrote. "The 1880s saw the collapse of civil rights for blacks as well as the publication of Huckleberry Finn. This collapse was an effort to bury the combustible issues Twain raised in his novel. The nation as well as Tom Sawyer, was deferring Jim's freedom in agonizing play. The cyclical attempts to remove the novel from classrooms extend Jim's captivity on into each generation of readers."

That's Toni Morrison, one helluva writer. Ages apart, from different worlds and lives, and Twain's words ring true to each one like a church bell. Throw off those shackles, folks. Read the book.

Appendix A: Two Critical Responses to *Huckleberry Finn*

Author's note: One of the wonderful things about teaching Huck is reading some of our finest writers on Twain's classic. Perhaps my favorite recent piece on the book was written by the terrific George Saunders. Mr. Saunders was every bit as kind and graceful in his email exchanges with me as he is on the page. My students really enjoyed this. It was very kind of him to permit me to include it here.

"The United States of Huck": Introduction to *Adventures of Huckleberry Finn*

GEORGE SAUNDERS

Introduction to the Introduction

Let me begin by confessing that I have had more trouble with this piece than I've ever had writing anything in my life, mainly because I love this book and was deathly afraid I would fail to do it justice, which causes me to rush off to the library and do hours and hours of research, which only terrified me further and reduced me to writing quaking tautological sentences like "Much has been written about the fact that, whereas the shores of the Mississippi, mythologically speaking, represent America's violence, the center of the river, which traditionally has been represented as Utopian, is also occasionally see to contain bloated floating corpses." Recognizing that my sentences were perhaps not as clear as they could be, I began furiously editing, bearing in mind at every instant that *Adventures of Huckleberry Finn* is probably the greatest and certainly the most influential American novel of all time and has inspired feelings of fierce love and loyalty in every important American writer, except in those other important American writers who have really, really disliked it and found it morally problematic, and soon I had worked myself into such a state of

Appendix A

bowing obeisance and timidity that my sentences became a bland series of tenuous apologetic nouns, no verbs at all, as these, I felt, were too risky.

But luckily that phase is past, and I can now, using quite a number of verbs, espouse a Tentative Narrative Theory regarding *Huck Finn.*

A Tentative Narrative Theory Regarding Huck Finn

Have you ever been in an airport and seen those escalators whose purpose it is to not actually escalate, but to move people horizontally, which is why they are called people movers? Imagine the novelist as a person standing at one end of a people mover, with a shovel, in front of a big pile of dirt. This pile of dirt represents The Thing This Writer Loves to Do, and Does Naturally. The writer started writing so that he or she could endlessly and effortlessly do this thing and nothing else—be funny, say, or verbally brilliant, or write lush nature vignettes, or detailed descriptions of the interiors of rich people's houses—and then be declared Wonderful and buy a nicer car. But all writers soon find that their Dirt is not enough. Yes, their readership stands at the far end of the people mover, eagerly awaiting this Dirt, but if the writer simply dumps shovelful after shovelful of Dirt onto the people mover, the people mover grinds to a halt, and the readership walks away to see a movie. Three hundred pages of descriptions of rich people's houses will not cut it; the writer must connect the dots of Dirt with something else, something narrative, something that imitates forward motion. The people mover must be fed Dirt a little at a time, so that it will keep moving, and in this way, and this way only, the readership will in time receive all the Dirt the writer wishes to administer.

Now to extend this already rickety metaphor, let us say that what keeps the people mover moving is what we will call the Apparent Narrative Rationale. The Apparent Narrative Rationale is what the writer and the reader have tacitly agree the book is "about." In most cases, the Apparent Narrative Rationale is centered around simply curiosity; the reader understands that he is waiting to learn if Scrooge will repent, if Romeo will marry Juliet, if the crops will be saved, the widow rescued. While the reader waits for that answer, the writer gets a chance to create the Three Christmas Ghosts and compose the Balcony Speech, and in the end, the reader finds that this—the Dirt—is what he or she has wanted all along.

Two Critical Responses to Huckleberry Finn

The Apparent Narrative Rationale, then, can be seen as the writer's answer to his own question: "What exactly is it that I am doing here?"

I now skillfully segue back to Mark Twain, aka Samuel Clemens.

Twain is the funniest literary American writer, and his funniness is so energetic and true and pure that is must have been a great pleasure to be him, sitting there dressed all in white, smoking cigar after cigar in your hexagonal study, with the pure funniness pouring out of the top of your head, helping you combat your native grouchiness. Like many lower-class writers (Chekhov, Dickens, Gogol come to mind) he started his career being purely funny, in comic sketches that were mostly Dirt and very little people mover, and all his writing life struggled with the question of what his Apparent Narrative Rationale should be, which is why he left behind such a long trail of abandoned manuscripts. He was not an outline, not a planner, did not establish an agenda and carry it through, but wrote as the spirit moved him, in as improvisatory a manner as any writer ever did. "Mr. Clemens," wrote William Dean Howells, his friend and editor, "is the first writer to use in extended writing the fashion we all use in thinking, and to set down the thing that comes into his mind without fear or favor of the thing that went before or the thing that may be about to follow.... (H)e would take whatever offered itself to his hand out of that mystical chaos, that divine ragbag, which we call the mind, and leave the reader to look after relevancies and sequences for himself."

Huck Finn was written in three or four distinct bursts of creativity, between which Twain put the manuscript away and wrote plays no one has ever heard of and invented machines no one has ever used. Each time he stopped, he apparently did so for the simplest of reasons: he didn't know how to keep going. He lost faith in his Apparent Narrative Rationale, or interest in it, or found it had led him to some seemingly insoluble narrative problem, and so put the book aside and invented an Invisible Ink Typewriter or a Systematic Noodle Identifier. Each time he came back to the book, he did so with renewed enthusiasm and a new plan on how to proceed: a new Apparent Narrative Rationale. This sequence of Apparent Narrative Rationales may be roughly described as follows: (1.) I Will Rewrite *Tom Sawyer*, but from Huck's Point of View; (2.) I Will Take Huck and Jim up the River, Ostensibly to Freedom; (3.) I Will Write a Treatise on the Mores and Manners of the American Southwest; (4.) I Will Build This Whole Deal Up into One of the Most Beautiful Moments of Impending Action Ever, in Which We See That Huck Must Risk His Life to Single-

Appendix A

handedly Save Jim; and (5.) I Will Let Tom Sawyer Come Inexplicably Back into My Story and Ruin My Ending.

Now, all fiction writers labor under this burden of not-knowing. "The writer," said Donald Barthelme, "is one who, embarking upon a task, does not know what to do." In this mode of not-knowing, the thick-torsoed, literal, and crew-cut conscious mind is move to the sidelines in favor of the swinging, perceptive, light-footed, tutu-wearing subconscious. We surprise ourselves, and make something bigger than we could have imagined making before we started trying to make it. But as Twain wrote *Huck Finn*, his not-knowing seems also to have been operating on a second and more profound level. All those adjustments of his Apparent Narrative Rationale took place in part because his book was making him uncomfortable. His comic novel was doing things a comic novel was not supposed to do, and yet he sort of liked it, and yet, come to think of it, it was really pretty darn uncomfortable, and he didn't yet feel like fighting the battles his story was presaging. In effect, his subconscious was urging him to do things his conscious mind didn't know could be done, or didn't particularly want done, and so my Tentative Narrative Theory is simply this: the tension between various warring parts of Sam Clemens—the radical and reactionary; the savage satirist and the kindly Humorist; the raw hick and the aspiring genteel Literary Figure—is what makes *Huck Finn* such a rich and formidable book.

That is all the narrative theory I have at the moment, but I will return to this question of Twain's understanding of his own book later, after I dispense with the question of whether *Huck Finn* is indeed a Great Novel or if, on the other hand, the millions of people who have read and loved it and felt that it was morally important and gorgeous have all been stupid and deceived and hopelessly old-fashioned and dupable.

What's So Great About It?

Twain started the book in 1876, as a companion piece to one he had recently finished, *The Adventures of Tom Sawyer*, but with a critical difference: he would tell the new story from the point of view of its main character, Huck Finn, son of the town drunk. "I shall take a boy of twelve & run him through life (in the first person)," Twain wrote to Howells in 1875. This first-person voice turned out to be one of the most natural and

Two Critical Responses to Huckleberry Finn

poetic literary voices ever devised, a voice still startling in its ability to bring the physical world (predawn birdcalls, a tin drainpipe on a moonlit night, the mud-smell of a river at dawn) off the page and into our heads, making us feel as if we hadn't merely read the scenes but lived them, over and over, in some parallel and primal universe. It is this voice that first gets us and it is this feeling of love for the voice—our delight in Huck's common sense, his original way of thinking, the perfect roll and cadence of these odd sentences, so unliterary by the standards of Twain's time—that first, I expect, put into some early critic's head the idea that the book was not just a boy's book, not just a quasi-naughty work of low comedy, but in fact, a great and seminal work of art. With this voice, Twain threw open the door on an America previously unrepresented in our literature: its lower classes, its hustlers and religious con men, possessed of equal parts Spirit and Lust: its leaning frame houses, inside of which corpulent men, tended by slaves, read aloud from Bibles. In an era when Whitman and Emerson were linking the health of the American democracy to its downward inclusiveness, along came *Huck Finn*, which was so terrifically downwardly inclusive that it was banned by the Concord Library for "dealing with a series of experiences not elevating."

The voice is what hooks so many young writers on the book and inspires them to attempt to do for our time what Twain did for his, which is why every few years there appears some new work described as "a *Huck Finn*-like reverie on freedom and constraint, set in a convent, in which Sister Gertrude, like Huck, dreams of climbing out the window and having a smoke" or "like *Huck Finn*, if Huck Finn was raised in Cleveland and Pap was not a cruel drunk but sort of a cranky rabbi." But this tendency of *Huck Finn* to cause other writer to write books extremely similar to it but worse is telling; the voice of the book reminds us of the beauty of the world, and of the fact that beauty can indeed be gotten at by the word, and that our language, English, that old dowager, has not yet begun to fight. As long as there is a new reality, the voice tells us, English too will be new, and it is you, the young writer, who will make it so. And so off the young writers go, trying to figure out what their River is, and who their Jim is, and what American's most current noxious trait is, so they can lampoon it. And although—at least the three or four times I've tried it—the final product is not a book at all, but a pile of papers you fling across the room: the final product is also a new respect for the originality and genius of the book, and for Twain, of whom F. Scott Fitzgerald once said,

Appendix A

beautifully: "His eyes were the first eyes that ever looked at us objectively that were not eyes from overseas."

In *Huck Finn*, the landscape appears to us on a strangely human scale; we feel ourselves actually moving through it. I don't know if this is true for anybody else, but when I read, my inner eye is normally situated about ten feet off the ground. I look down on Dostoevsky's characters as if perched beside some icon on a beet-smelling shelf; when Bob Cratchit tests the Christmas pudding, I'm up on the stove, which fortunately for me is one of those instantaneously cooling Victorian stoves. When I read *Huck Finn* though, I am Huck's height, looking up at all these unkempt hostile people looking down at me, grazing a tree with my arm, running a finger through the dust that has settled on an end table in that magnificently described Grangerford parlor, killing an actual pig, letting the hand that killed the pig trail behind me in the green waters of the Mississippi.

The person who tries to list all that is wonderful about *Huck Finn* will soon find that his family has fled, the grass has overgrown the sidewalk, the dog has starved to death, and his life is over. There is wonderfulness everywhere you look, and from whatever angle you look. I would guess that a person could wade into the book with any idea in mind ("Christianity," or "the forest," or "concepts of feminine beauty") and find that idea not only represented in *Huck Finn* but metaphorically developed, and metaphorically developed in a way that simultaneously sheds light on Twain, the reader, and the cosmos. Try it yourself: read it, say with "concepts of feminine beauty" in mind, and you will soon find yourself convinced that Twain only invented the stuff about the kid and the slave and the big river and freedom and democracy as a diversionary tactic so he could really sink his teeth into the concept of feminine beauty.

Such metaphorical suppleness comes, I think, in proportion to how purely the artistic produce proceeds from the subconscious, and from the quality of that subconscious. Twain's subconsciousness was a formidable thing—he had been just about everywhere in America, usually at a time when something big was happening, had done that most purely American thing, namely work himself above his original station, had begun his life as a lower middle-class kid in a slave-owning household, which situated him squarely on the twin issues that make every American sweat and frown and burst into defensiveness and begin spouting groundless platitudes, namely race and class—and when this subconscious took charge, emboldened by a temporarily perplexed conscious mind, the book wrote itself out of any known genre and into this wild new thing we are still trying to classify and make sense of.

So there is the voice, and the created world along the river, and the amazing assortment of characters, and the constantly shifting skein of metaphors, and the rich stinging humor—but what truly animates the book, and makes it so dangerous and transcendent and even prescient, is the relationship between Huck and Jim.

The Central Moral Vector

Huck is an ignorant white-trash boy. Not only is he white trash, he is the lowest of the white trash, sort of White-Trash. Trash, because his father is the town drunk. And this town drunk is not of the Amiable Nostalgic school of town drunkery but of the Brutal Violent school. Huck flees town to escape Pap and the equally oppressive if less flamboyant Righteous Spinster Duo, Miss Watson and the Widow Douglas, and soon is faced with a dilemma; this dilemma is named Jim, and Jim is an escaped slave, and all of Huck's training thus far has been that slavery is good, biblically sanctioned even, and that he should always do what is right, which in this case means he should turn Jim in. Bearing in mind our human fondness for establishing ourselves as Worthwhile by kicking someone beneath us simply because we can, especially if we ourselves have been repeatedly kicked. It would not be surprising if Huck, who has no mother and no real home and a father who locks him in a shed and beats him, were to take a little pleasure from mistreating Jim. (Imagine a sort of contemporary Huck-equivalent: a little community-despised white-trash boy, son of an American Nazi Party member who periodically beats him and locks him in the garage for days, comes upon a sleeping and vulnerable homeless black man—what might he do?) And yet all of Huck's instincts tell him that Jim is a man, and a friend, and we come to see that Jim cares about Huck more genuinely, with more real affection, than anyone else in the book, and so the Central Moral Vector lies in the question: Will Huck turn Jim in?

Huck struggles with this question, and watching this struggle we come to love him, and conducting this struggle, he becomes one of the great figures of world literature. "No one who reads thoughtfully the dialectic of Huck's moral crisis," Lionel Trilling said, "will ever again be

Appendix A

wholly able to accept without some question and some irony the assumptions of the respectable morality by which he lives."

Anyway, this is what we are told, and taught, and what we remember about the book years later, the book is about the question of whether Huck, this probably nascent racist, will transcend himself and help Jim realize his dream of freedom. This question hangs over the entire book and, to the contemporary mind gives it the shape that allows us to argue for its noble moral intent, and to assess its artistic triumph or failure, but the truth is, there are entire sections of the book that behave as if this question had not been asked. Jim spends a good deal of the middle portion of the book effectively neutralized as a narrative player, hidden on board the raft or in the woods, with his face painted blue and/or tied hand and foot and/or dressed up like King Lear. There are other places where Jim fades into caricature, and in these places it seems as if Twain—involved in the writing of the book and not in its analysis many years later, flailing around in search of his Apparent Narrative Rationale, still emerging from the slog of his childhood racial attitudes, trying on different models of what his book was, inventing and reinventing his Upside-Down Lapel Reinstator—has gotten what his book is about, or at least has forgotten what, many years later, we will claim his book is about.

All of what is debated and sometimes deplored about *Huck Finn* – its structural problems, its weak ending, its racism—can, I contend, be traced back to the fact that Twain only dimly and imperfectly understood that his book had a Central Moral Vector. Or rather, he knew, but sometimes forgot. Or rather, he knew, but periodically got interested in other aspects of the book and lost sight of it. Or maybe, and most interestingly, his Central Moral Vector was too hot to handle, and would have required him to simultaneously invent, understand, and complete his book in an entirely new genre, a genre that neither Twain nor the world was quite ready for.

The Ending, Oh My God, the Ending

> Author's note: I did not use this little section from Saunders' introduction in our first reading so as not to prejudice the students against the ending before they actually had read it. I did share it with them after we'd read Huck Finn and marked their responses. Unlike literary critics who were generally appalled by Twain's far-fetched finish, they were okay with Twain's ending.

Twain's failure to love, honor, and obey his Central Moral Vector is most gut-droppingly apparent in the ending. "In the whole reach of the English novel, there is not a more abrupt or chilling descent," wrote Bernard DeVoto, one of our great Twain scholars, and since we are heaping scorn on the ending, I may as well quote Leo Marx, another one of our great Twain scholars, who said that the ending "jeopardizes the significance of the entire novel." Even Hemingway, who loved the book, and whose famous quote about it ("All modern American literature comes from one book by Mark Twain called *Huckleberry Finn*. It's the best book we've had.... There was nothing before...") is required for any introduction (and so I have now discharged that duty, with apologies to Melville and Poe and Hawthorne, who might feel that their books had at least a little something to do with modern American literature)—even Hemingway suggested that the reader stop reading before the end of the book, which, since Hemingway is no longer with us and therefore cannot beat me up, I have to say strikes me as a bit of a cop-out: the book has an ending, and Twain loved that ending, and wrote it in what was basically a transport of ecstasy in the summer of 1876, sometimes working from breakfast to dinner, and never disclaimed it afterward but proudly and successfully read from it on the book's reading tour.

Having said all this, I will also say that there is a kind of perverse greatness in the ending, in the sense that Waterloo was a last great battle for someone as considerable as Napoleon. Some part of Twain realized what he had brought himself to the brink of, and great talent that he was, he did not tarry on the brink of that cliff, or pretend there was no cliff, or that he was standing at the edge of it: instead he ran at high speed back the way he'd come, causing a disaster, but one that is on as grand a scale as the novel itself.

So What's Wrong with It, Exactly?

For me, the most moving part of the book is the scene at the end of chapter 23. Jim tells Huck about the time he slapped his young daughter in the head for not obeying him, only to find that she had never actually heard him: she had gone deaf from a recent bout with scarlet fever. It's a heartbreaker, as I was reminded just now when I went to get the chapter reference, reread it, and started bawling. Any parent reading this is sickened

Appendix A

with the magnitude and hurtfulness of Jim's error, with the impossibility of ever really erasing it, and—this is a particular manifestation of Twain's moral genius—with the fact that, horrible as this mistake would have been for any parent, this parent is a slave, a thousand miles from a home he will probably never get back to, if the prevailing national culture has its way.

We leave this scene with our sense of the Central Moral Vector confirmed: Huck's dawning realization of Jim's humanity is essential to the story, and Twain knows it.

Eighty pages or so later, Huck finds out that Jim has been sold and is being imprisoned, and has to decide what to do. There follows one of the most famous and wonderful passages in any literature, in which Huck decides, finally, to purposely do what he knows to be wrong—free Jim—and thus doom himself to hell. It is a brilliant hymn to clear-sightedness and against hypocrisy, and when you read it with the memory of the above-mentioned scene still fresh in your mind, the effect is to be slingshotted toward what now feels like the inevitable ending: Huck, who has lied and tricked his way down the river, will now lie and trick Jim free, or will try to.

Twain has written himself into a tough and very serious spot. Jim is being held prisoner in the Deep South by people used to holding prisoners, people who do not hold wishy-washy opinions about slaves, or what to do with them, or what to do with people, even little boys, who help them escape. Three ideas, which Twain has skillfully nurtured throughout the book, come together, (1.) Huck has transcended himself; (2.) Jim is the best and most genuine human being in the book; and (3.) the violence that has been intensifying and coming closer to Jim and Huck throughout the novel is now nearly upon them. And suddenly we feel, as perhaps Twain did, that the book has written itself out of its rollicking comic tradition and into something else, something more tragic and frightening, that would indict America in a way America would not soon forget.

Because what should happen is something deeply sad. Jim cannot escape, not for long, and Huck cannot remain unpunished for having helped Jim escape; the country Twain has made is too cruel and sure of itself and methodical in its slavery for either of these things to happen. And Twain understood the book—as we do—to be a comic novel, and the prospect of Jim being sold down the river or lynched, and Huck being bullwhipped and/or sent to a reformatory, say, does not gibe with our expectations of a comic novel, where violence happens only to side players, and generally off-camera, and usually because they deserve it.

Two Critical Responses to Huckleberry Finn

So what does Twain do? This literary purist, who had lambasted James Fenimore Cooper for his too-lengthy canoes and exaggeratedly hearing-gifted Indians, commits one of the worst Coincidences in the history of writing. Huck approaches the house where Jim is being held, planning to enact another swindle, and a woman comes out, mistakes him for another little boy (we flinch a bit at this; mistaken identity has been used maybe once too often in this book), and then—horror of horrors—we learn that this other little boy's name is Tom, and we begin whispering to ourselves, *No way, no way, Mark, Sam—don't do it*—but our worst fears are soon confirmed: this woman is Tom Sawyer's aunt, and she—here, eleven hundred miles upriver—is expecting a visit from Tom himself *any minute now.*

Now, a coincidence is all right, life is full of them, but a reader's willingness to ingest one is inversely related to how badly the writer needs one, and Twain needed one very badly at this point, to avoid stepping into the dangerous trap his subconscious had set for him.

So at the moment when Huck seems most complete, heroic and alive, Tom Sawyer, that Europhile, that conceptualizer, that American Philistine, comes flying up the river to save Twain from his own book.

A Word About Tom, That Stinker

Tom Sawyer is likeable enough in *The Adventures of Tom Sawyer*, tolerable in the opening chapters of *Huck Finn*, where he serves mostly as a marker for how much more humane and sensible Huck is. In those early chapters, Huck grows increasingly skeptical of Tom's imitative and book-toadying and derivative style of adventure, and seemingly leaves him behind forever in the famous line, "It had all the marks of a Sunday School." Then it's out on the river for Huck, eleven hundred miles of adventure and tricks and self-reliance and encounters with grown men, from which he emerges triumphant, saved again and again by his own common sense and wit, while presumably Tom is back home, dipping pigtails in ink wells and whining about how Sid is teasing him too much and so forth.

The difference between Tom and Huck is that Huck believes in the reality of what he sees and feels, and Tom does not. Tom believes in what he has read in books, or, more correctly, in the concepts that have arisen from what he has read in books. Huck believes in the reality of the people

Appendix A

and things he sees, whereas to Tom, these things are only imperfect imitations of the people and things about which he has read. Because Huck believes that other people are real, he also believes in the reality of their suffering; he grieves when he hurts Jim, worries about the drunken rider at the circus, feels bad for betraying Miss Watson, and, most importantly, understands how much Jim needs his freedom. To Tom, Jim is not real, nor is Jim's suffering; Jim's suffering is simply an opportunity for Tom's ego and cleverness to exert themselves. He prolongs and worsens this suffering by putting Jim through an insane ritual of escape a la those in Walter Scott novels (the low-comic riff that was Twain's Apparent Narrative Rationale at that time) and by withholding from Jim the staggering truth: Jim has been free for most of the novel, because Miss Watson emancipated him on her deathbed.

Tom and Huck, of course, respond to different parts of their creator. Tom, perhaps, to that part of Twain that longed for acceptance from the Snooty East, and Superior Europe, and distrusted the Huck part—so crude, wild, backwoodsy, and unschooled. Literary characters can only come from their creator's psyche, but in this case—maybe because Twain's psyche was such a specimen psyche, and because he had such unfettered access to it—his personal binary was also a critical national one: Huck and Tom represent two viable models of the American Character. They exist side by side in every American and American action. America is, and always has been, undecided about whether it will be the United States of Tom or the United States of Huck. The United States of Tom looks at misery and says: Hey, I didn't do it. It looks at inequity and says: All my life I have busted my butt to get where I am, so don't come crying to me. Tom likes kings, codified nobility, unquestioned privilege. Huck likes people, fair play, spreading the truck around. Whereas Tom knows, Huck wonders. Whereas Huck hopes, Tom presumes. Whereas Huck cares, Tom denies. These two parts of the American Psyche have been at war since the beginning of the nation, and come to think of it, these two parts of the World Psyche have been at war since the beginning of the world, and the hope of the nation and of the world is to embrace the Huck part and send the Tom part back up the river where it belongs.

But this not what happens in *Huck Finn*.

Instead, Huck-Growing becomes Huck-Stultified. His clarity and moral resolve fade and he becomes, if anything, more of a passive Sawyer-lackey than he was at the beginning of the book. (Maria Konnikova's fascinating article for *Scientific American* was so interesting on this very point.) Jim falls off the shelf of the human entirely. He allows himself to be bitten by rats, writes notes on the wall in his own blood, does not escape though there is a clear route of escape, participates in Tom's idiotic rituals without a word of objection. Convinced of the holiness of Huck's mission, we are forced to watch that mission be reduced to a sickening vaudeville sketch.

"Having only half-escaped the genteel tradition, one of whose preeminent characteristics was an optimism undaunted by disheartening truth," Santayana wrote, "(Twain) returned to it."

Tom and Huck, of course, respond to different parts of their creator. Tom, perhaps, to that part of Twain that longed for acceptance from the Snooty East, and Superior Europe, and distrusted the Huck part—so crude, wild, backwoodsy, and unschooled. Literary characters can only come from their creator's psyche, but in this case—maybe because Twain's psyche was such a specimen psyche, and because he had such unfettered access to it—his personal binary was also a critical national one: Huck and Tom represent two viable models of the American Character. They exist side by side in every American and American action. America is, and always has been, undecided about whether it will be the United States of Tom or the United States of Huck. The United States of Tom looks at misery and says: Hey, I didn't do it. It looks at inequity and says: All my life I have busted my butt to get where I am, so don't come crying to me. Tom likes kings, codified nobility, unquestioned privilege. Huck likes people, fair play, spreading the truck around. Whereas Tom knows, Huck wonders. Whereas Huck hopes, Tom presumes. Whereas Huck cares, Tom denies. These two parts of the American Psyche have been at war since the beginning of the nation, and come to think of it, these two parts of the World Psyche have been at war since the beginning of the nation, and come to think of it, these two parts of the World Psyche have been at war since the beginning of the world, and the hope of the nation and of the world is to embrace the Huck part and send the Tom part back up the river, where it belongs.

But this is not what happens in *Huck Finn*.

Instead, Huck-Growing becomes Huck-Stultified. His clarity and moral resolve fade and he becomes, if anything, more of a passive Sawyer-lackey than he was at the beginning of the book. Jim falls off the shelf of the human entirely. He allows himself to be bitten by rats, writes notes on

Appendix A

the wall in his own blood, does not escape though there is a clear route of escape, participates in Tom's idiotic rituals without a word of objection. Convinced of the holiness of Huck's mission, we are forced to watch that mission reduced to a sickening vaudeville sketch.

"Having only half-escaped the genteel tradition, one of whose preeminent characteristics was an optimism undaunted by disheartening truth," Santayana wrote, (Twain) returned to it."

Let's Burn It, Then Ban It, Then Burn It Again

Even before its publication, *Huck Finn* was at the center of a controversy involving one of its illustrations, which had been changed by an ornery typographer who put a certain part of Uncle Silas's anatomy rather than inside them, and made it look something like an angry duck. Original objections to the book itself centered around the issue of its crudeness. The book itself was a shocking portrayal of a white-trash boy who smoked, snuck out windows barefoot, sat around naked on a raft, smokes some more, told a bunch of lies, then openly expressed desire to go to hell. Over the years, as the much-feared epidemic of young boys sneaking out of windows barefoot while smoking and wishing to go to hell never materialized, the crudity objection faded, replaced by another; the book and its author were racist. Or maybe just the book was racist. Or maybe the author was partly racist, which infected the book, which basically had its heart in the right place.

In *Mark Twain and His Times*, Arthur G. Pettit paints a picture of Twain as a man who started out life a natural, enculturated racist and gradually grew out of it or as out of it as his time and culture permitted. Twain was the son of a slave owner, in a town of slave owners. As a boy, he saw his father administer beatings and floggings and once saw a fellow townsman crush a slave's head with an iron bar. Near the real-life model for Huck Finn's Jackson Island, young Clemens found the disemboweled body of a murdered slave, and at fourteen, he witnessed the lynching of a black man accused of raping a white woman. Before and during the time of the Civil War, according to Pettit, Twain 'ranted against 'niggers' and told a long series of popular jokes about 'nigger odor,' fried 'nigger' steaks, black promiscuity, and the evils of miscegenation." But by the 1880's, Twain had changed; he made impassioned speeches against race brutality, paid the Yale tuition of several black students, became friends with Frederick Douglass and Booker T. Washington. In short, his natural clearheadedness asserted itself on the issue of racial equality, and it was out of this spirit that *Huck Finn* came.

But given Twain's roots, it would be surprising if the book's representation of blacks didn't bear some evidence of its author's journey. And it does. There are moments, even before the ending, when the "real" Jim—that is, the Jim we perceive through, or in spite of, Huck's foreshortened first-person presentation of him is not fully human but a minstrelish caricature, moments when we sense that somewhere in the back of Twain's mind, some swaggering remnant of the Hannibal kid is cranking out stereotypical comic images of blacks for cheat laughs, images that Twain the Reformed is failing to fully reject. It is wholly appropriate that Jim be a believable slave, subject to all the restrictions, educational and otherwise, that that word implies but there is no need for him to be an idiot. And there are places in the book where Jim is presented as simpleminded, almost retarded, and these places are in stark contrast to other places where we see him as an intelligent, kind, wary, adult runaway, doing his best to balance his natural goodness against his fear of recapture, his justifiable suspicion of Huck against his real affection for the boy.

The questions about race in *Huck Finn* tend to center around the presence in the book of the word "nigger," but my guess is that, if the book were free of the types of missteps described above, and if the ending weren't such a fiasco, that word might not be such a problem. That is, if our wishful dream of the book (in which Jim is always fully human and three-dimensional, and in which Huck steadily and then definitively comes to understand this) had been perfectly realized, I think most readers would tolerate the *n*-word as an important and even essential indicator of character. It is crucial that we understand Huck as a possible nascent racist, and so he had better talk like one. Imagine a story about the possible salvation of a young misogynist, son of a radical woman-hater, the story is nonsense if that budding misogynist and his creepy father speak of women only in the purest and most enlightened terms.

Having said that, I will also say that a writer who uses the *n*-word (which even in Twain's day was understood to be derogatory) walks a fine moral line. He or she can do one of three things with the n-word (or other ethnic slurs, or gender pejoratives): (1) use it less than it could "actually" be used, that is, omit or decrease its use by people who might be reasonable

Appendix A

be expected, by virtue of their class or education or stupidity, to use it; (2) use it exactly as much as it "should" be used, that is, use it whenever it seems that a given character would indeed use it, and when its use is thematically essential; or (3) use it more than it would actually be used, that is, use it gratuitously, swaggeringly. Which was Twain doing? Was Twain swaggering? Do we detect any swaggering? If so, is this possible apparent swaggering only an accurate imitation of the actual ambient swaggering of his boyhood Hannibal? At this point in the argument, one starts to get a nauseated bean-countery feeling: Can we ever really know to what extent this man or his book was, or is, racist? When we identify racism in the book, aren't we really just identifying racism in the culture out of which it came? Is it fair to expect Twain to have vaulted himself out of his time and place and arrive, clean-booted and upright, in our own? Isn't the book still funny and deep? Aren't I actually enjoying it? How does one do the complicated math of Ultimate Racism: If we determine that relative to our time, Twain was a 40 percent racist, while relative to his own, he was only a 12 percent racism, or was in fact a 0 percent racist—what do we know, really?

And yet the question of race in *Huck Finn* matters very much, if you are the young black man or woman who, reading the book, is made uncomfortable or ashamed by it, or if, conversely, you are the young white man or woman who, reading the book, has some secret feelings or race superiority inflamed. It matters a lot and it is very complicated. That the book is beautiful and thrilling is undeniable. That parts of it make the contemporary reader queasy is also undeniable. That the book and its author had an antiracist intent is also undeniable. That the author did not fulfill that intent as purely as he would have, had he been born in our time rather than his own, but with the exact same talent, having had exactly the same life experiences, is also undeniable, as well as completely nonsensical. We got Twain when we got him, and thank goodness we did, and God help the culture that pretends that earlier stupidities never happened and tries to eradicate all evidence of them.

Maybe the best we can do is concede that the book is beautiful and difficult, and that its beauties and its difficulties are inseparably linked, and then try to understand (and teach) that the book's racial problems can be dissected and understood narratively—that is, in terms of how stories are told and received—and that we are all empowered by the process of undertaking this sort of investigation.

Two Critical Responses to Huckleberry Finn

The problems with race in *Huck Finn* can best be understood as narrative problems, technical problems, and the process of discerning and understanding these technical problems is a noble process, and the ability to discern and understand these problems is an essential ability. In a culture that is becoming ever more story-stupid, in which a representative of the Coca-Cola company can, with a straight face, pronounce, as he donates a collection of archival Coca-Cola commercials to the Library of Congress, that "Coca-Cola has become an integral part of people's lives by helping to tell these stories," it is perhaps not surprising that people have trouble teaching and receiving a novel as complex and flawed as *Huck Finn*, but it is even more urgent that we learn to look passionately and technically at stories, if only to protect ourselves from the false and manipulative ones being circulated among us.

At Last I'm Done, and You Can Go Read It

Art, at its best, is a kind of uncontrolled yet disciplined Yelp, made by one of us who, because of the brain he was born with and the experiences he has had and the training he has received, is able to emit a Yelp that contains all of the joys, miseries, and contradictions of life as it is actually lived. That Yelp, which is not a logical sound, does good for all of us. Chekhov said that the purpose of art is not to solve problems but to formulate them correctly, and in *Huck Finn,* Twain formulated our national problems in a joyful and madly funny and frightening Yelp that amounted to a national clearing of the throat. It is kind of insane, this book, but in the same way that tribal cultures immunize and strengthen themselves by sitting around spouting descriptions of his mad vision, we are improved by Twain's great Yelp: it contains, in capsule form, all that is very right and very wrong with us, and amounts to a complex equation proving that our right and our wrong both proceed out of the same national energy. If the Yelp is a bit rough, off-pitch, and inconsistent in places, God bless him: at least he did it.

As I've worked on this piece, an image has sometimes come to mind of Twain standing outside a jail, and inside the jail is A True American Literature. Twain, wearing, maybe, a top hat, takes a top hat, takes a good hard crazy run at it, and knocks the shack down, and a True American Literature is suddenly free to wander about in the world. In the process,

Appendix A

Twain's hat is knocked awry, and his nose is broken, and pretty soon a crowd gathers, saying "Jeez, Mark, your hat's crooked and your nose is broken and your ending stinks and your book seems a little racist"—but damn it, there's that fallen shack, and a True American Literature is now sauntering off into the woods, being eagerly tracked by all those Hungry American Writers, who have included, over the years, Salinger and Ellison and Faulkner and Hemingway and Morrison and Eliot and Bellow and Carver. Twain sacrificed his hat and his nose so the rest of us would have something good to track, and track it, we have, all these years, and the tracking of it has helped us, I would argue, confront the very issues that make the book problematic: racism, timidity, denial, our national urge-to-the-genteel.

Twain would like this, I think, this continuing struggle to understand his book. We have not had a writer as devoted to seeing out truth and outing lies. *Huck Finn* is a great book because it tells the truth about the human condition in a way that delights us. It is a great work of our national literature because, more than any book before or since, it locates itself squarely on our National Dilemma, which is: How can anyone be truly free in a country as violent and stupid as ours? The book lives, because the question does.

"Is *Huckleberry Finn's* Ending Really Lacking? Not If You're Talking Psychology"

MARIA KONNIKOVA

Author's note: The funny thing about this article is I just happened to see Maria Konnikova on Real Time *with Bill Maher a day before I found her deeply engaging and thoughtful article online. It makes such perfect sense—why not ask a psychologist about Huck's behavior? Wouldn't he know more about how a teenager would act then some book critic? Ms. Konnikova was, again, extraordinarily gracious about permitting me to use the article. Thanks to her. I wish more Twain scholars and critics would read this.*

Originally published in Scientific American *on October 5, 2012. The views expressed are those of Maria Konnikova and are not necessarily those of* Scientific American.

Two Critical Responses to Huckleberry Finn

The Adventures of Huckleberry Finn: one of Mark Twain's most famous novels. In fact, probably one of the most famous English-language novels of all time, period. And certainly, one of the most frequent contenders to that elusive berth of the Great American Novel. With one caveat, that is. Many readers, reviewers, and critics over the year have found fault with Twain's ending. It's not worthy of the book, they argue.

Even T. S. Eliot and Lionel Trilling—the two most vocal proponents of *Huck Finn*'s iconic status—had to explain it away. And what's more, they continue, it's completely unmotivated psychologically. How could Huck, after building a friendship with Jim for the duration of the book, after deepening his connection and realizing how much more there is to the man than the category "slave," just turn around and forget him like that? How can he fall back so easily into old habits, as if he hadn't grown at all from start to finish? It doesn't make sense.

I won't argue for or against the ending's artistic merits. That's a topic for another piece. But what I will say is that psychologically, Huck's about-face couldn't be more sound. Twain might have offended on other accounts, but there is one thing he got right: not only *could* Huck fall back to old ways at the tip of a hat—or the arrival of a Tom Sawyer, as the case may be—but he most likely *would* do so if he were a flesh-and-blood twelve year old fresh off a rafting adventure.

What is it exactly that critics of the novel's final chapters object to? Jane Smiley sums up the arguments in a 1996 piece for *Harper's*. "It is with the feud that the novel begins to fail, because from here on the episodes are a mere distraction to the true subject of the work: Huck's affection for and responsibility to Jim." Huck cares little that Jim might be dead when the two are separated in the fog. He doesn't seem much affected when he discovers, at last, that Jim is alive after all. And that's not to mention the worst offence of all: Huck's behavior once he reunites with his old partner in crime, Tom Sawyer. As Leo Marx put it in a 1953 essay, when Tom enters the picture, Huck falls "almost completely under his sway once more, and we are asked to believe that the boy who felt pity for the rogues is now capable of making Jim's capture the occasion for a game. He becomes Tom's helpless accomplice, submissive and gullible." And to Marx, this regressive transformation is as unforgiveable as it is unbelievable.

From a literary standpoint, perhaps it is unforgiveable; it is not for me, here, to judge. But psychologically, the reversion is as sound as it gets,

Appendix A

despite the fury that it inspires. Before we rush to judge Huck—and to criticize Twain for veering so seemingly off course—we'd do well to consider a few key elements of the situations. First, Huck is a thirteen (or thereabouts)-year-old boy. He is, in other words, a teenager. What's more, he is a teenager from the antebellum South. Add to that the disparity between his social standing and education and Tom Sawyer's, and you get a picture of someone who is quite different from a righteous fifty-something (or even thirty-something) literary critic who is writing in the twentieth century for a literary audience. And that someone has to be judged appropriately for his age, background, and social context—and his creator, evaluated accordingly. Peer pressure is an incredibly powerful force, no matter your age. In general, we tend to care—and care desperately at that—what other people think of us. Numerous studies have shown educated, intelligent people acting in bizarre ways just to fit in with a group of completely unknown individuals—and ones they are not likely to ever again encounter.

In a series of classic studies of conformity, Solomon Asch found that people would disbelieve their eyes and go along with group consensus when judging the length of lines, even when the group consensus was obviously wrong. (The effect isn't a weak one. It has been replicated over the years with things like areas of figures, number series and other logical completions, vocabulary, and so on.) It didn't take much for them to change their mind if the group seemed to lean in a different direction.

Now, let's go back to Huck for a moment. There are a few important issues at play. Huck is not an adult. Tom Sawyer is not a stranger. The South is not a psychology lab. And slavery is not a bunch of lines projected on a screen. Each one of these factors on its own is enough to complicate the situation immensely—and together, they create one big complicated mess, that makes it increasingly likely that Huck will act just as he does, by conforming to Tom's wishes and reverting to their old group dynamic. Let's take the question of age. As it turns out, even though peer pressure is ubiquitous and conformity, a powerful force, there are certain ages where the dynamic peaks. One classic set of studies from 1979 looked at over 500 children from the 3rd, 6th, 9th, and 11th or 12th grades and examined their tendency to conform to both peers and parents on a range of behaviors. What the researchers found was that conformity to peers followed a non-linear pattern: it peaked in the 6th (median age just over 12) or 9th (median age just over 15) grade, depending on the type of behavior—the antisocial behavioral conformity peaked, on average, later than conformity to other behaviors—and then decreased by 11th and 12th grade (median age 18). But that's not the whole story. When the researchers looked at conformity to parents, they found a steady decrease in conforming behavior. Indeed, for the majority of measures, peer and parental conformity were negatively correlated. And what's more, the sharpest decline was in conformity to pro-social behaviors. Why is the parental trend important? Jim is an adult—and an adult who has become a whole lot like a parent to Huck throughout their adventures, protecting him and taking care of him (and later, of Tom as well) much as a parent would. And the behavior that he wants from Huck, when he wants anything at all, is prosocial in the extreme (an apology, to take the most famous example, for playing a trick on him in the fog; not much of an ask, it seems, unless you stop to consider that it's a slave asking a white boy to acknowledge that he was in the wrong). Tom, on the other hand, is a peer. And his demands are far closer to the anti-social side of the scale. Is it so surprising, then, that Huck sides with his old mate? The behavior becomes even understandable when we add in a few more variables. Another crucial caveat to Huck's apparent metamorphosis: we tend to behave differently in private versus public spheres. Context in large part determines how we act. A closed-door us is not the same as the us that faces the world in a social setting. As psychologists from George Kelly on have argued, behavior is highly contextual—especially when it comes to behaviors that may not be as socially acceptable as one might hope. Huck and Jim's raft is akin to a private sphere. It is just them, alone on the river, social context flowing away. And when does Huck's behavior start to shift? The moment that he returns to a social environment, when he joins the Grangerfords in their family feud. With the arrival of Tom, that change is even more apparent: Tom is a part of Huck's past, and there is nothing like context to cue us back to past habitual behavior in a matter of minutes. (That's one of the reasons, incidentally, that drug addicts often revert back to old habits when back in old environments.) Again, then, is it all that surprising that Huck reverts back to his old self, shedding some of the change that was inspired by the Mississippi? And the trajectory is true of Jim just as much as it is of Huck. In the same essay where he laments Huck's fall from heroic grace to Tom Sawyer's old sidekick, Marx comments on Jim's problematic decline as well: "It should be added at once that Jim doesn't mind [the change in Huck] too much. The fact is that he has undergone a similar transformation. On

Appendix A

the raft he was an individual, man enough to denounce Huck when Huck made him the victim of a practical joke. In the closing episode, however, we lose sight of Jim in the maze of farcical invention." On the raft, Jim was in a new environment, where old rules need not apply—especially given its private nature. But how quickly old ways kick back in, irrespective of whether you were a Huck or a Jim in that prior context. Smiley takes her criticism on this point a step further: there is a chasm, she points out, between Huck's stated affection for Jim and his willingness to then act on it, especially in these final episodes. She blames the divide on Twain's racism. But wouldn't it be more correct to blame Huck's only too real humanity? It's that same break between the private and the public, the new and the habitual. All too often, there is a disconnect between feeling, what we say, and action, what we do about it. And that is especially true when we step on moral ground that conflicts with accepted public practice (the Red Scare comes immediately to mind for me here). Marx and Smiley agree on one point: by the end of the book, "[m]ost of those traits which made [Huck] so appealing as a hero now disappear." And that may be their main beef with Twain's choice of ending. But here's the thing. You don't have to hold Huck as a hero if you don't want to. What you can't then go out and do is deny his reality—and criticize Twain's depiction of his actions and choices. Twain doesn't make Huck a hero. He makes him real. Can we blame the book for telling it like it is? *Huckleberry Finn*'s reality may not be what we *want* or what would make the book morally satisfying—but it is all too easy to understand in human terms. In those last chapters, Twain wasn't taking an easy way out or wrapping up loose ends any which way he could. He was showing us ourselves as we actually are—as we change from the private (river) to the public (town) sphere, when of a sudden, others' eyes are on us. And that is not a pretty sight to behold.

Appendix B: Selected Short Works by Twain, with Annotations

Author's note: For the teacher hoping to ease students into the world and work of Mark Twain, the three pieces below offer starting points. Each is brief and entertaining while also incorporating certain hallmarks of Twain's writing, including a few that readers will encounter repeatedly in Huckleberry Finn. *Either bracketed annotations within or questions and commentary following these short works suggest points of discussion. This author has provided a [commentary] here and there.*

"Private Habits of Horace Greeley" —Nov. 1868

(Originally published in the Spirit of the Times, *a New York City weekly.) Author's note: Even if you're a Mark Twain fan, chances are, you've never read this little-known, seldom anthologized romp. To me, what better way to introduce Twain's style and scalawag attitude to young readers. I came upon it in a valuable Charles Neider collection of Twain's journalism called "Life As I Find It." I found it irresistible and I think students will, too.*

At the time of this article, which was written for a weekly newspaper called The *Spirit of the Times*, Horace Greeley—the target of this spoof—was the editor of the *New York Tribune* and a genuine American celebrity. Greeley might have been the most influential newspaper man of the moment.

A devout abolitionist, his famous editorial called "The Prayer Of Twenty Millions" in August 1862 tried to shame President Abraham Lincoln into taking stronger action. The editorial inspired a famous—and rare–Presidential response: "If I could save the Union without freeing any slave, I would do it; "Lincoln wrote. "And if I could save it by freeing all the slaves, I would do it; and if I could save it by freeing some and leaving others alone, I would also do that."

Since we'll be getting into the issue of slavery anyway, this is a subtle way to bring up the subject and also show how Twain was not afraid to take on a bold topic, something we want to encourage in the students.

Appendix B

Clearly, Greeley was an important figure in American life, a journalist with considerable power and influence, probably not somebody that a little-known, first-time book author ought to screw around with. Greeley was not known for a sense of humor and, in a way, was Twain's boss, since Greeley's newspaper, The *New York Herald-Tribune* was one of the newspapers who helped pay for Twain's Holy Land tour that resulted in his first book, *Innocents Abroad*. Just four years later, Greeley would run for President against Ulysses S. Grant and get whomped.

Somehow, Twain found him a perfect target. His first book, *Innocents Abroad*, was just out. He was just getting a taste of celebrity, enjoying the response, finding a way to tug on everyone's sleeve. Looking back, he was fearless, bold, playful. Aren't these attributes you'd want in your budding young writers? So let's look at how Twain told us about the dignified Horace Greeley.

"Private Habits of Horace Greeley" (Mark Twain)

An intimate acquaintance with a distant relative [*your source is who?*] of the editor of the Tribune puts it in my power to furnish the public with the last—positively the very last [*sarcasm note*]—link necessary to perfect the chain of knowledge already in its possession concerning Mr. Greeley: I mean his private habits. We know all about as regards every other department of his life and service. Because, whenever a magazinist or a bookmaker is employed to writer, and cannot think of subject, he writes about Horace Greeley. Even the boys in the schools have quit building inspired "compositions" on "The Horse," and have gone to doing Horace Greeley instead; and when declamation-day comes around, their voices are no longer "still for war" and Patrick Henry, but for peace and Horace Greeley. [*Think Twain is a little annoyed at how famous Greeley had become?*] Now the natural result of all this is that the public have come at last to think that this man has no life but public life, no nature but a public nature, no habits but public habits. This is all wrong. [*Correct the record, Mr. Twain*] Mr. Greeley has a private life. Mr. Greeley has private habits.

Mr. Greeley gets up at three o'clock in the morning; for it is one of his favorite maxims that only early rising can keep the health unimpaired and the brain vigorous. He then wakes up all the household and assembles them in the library, by candle-light; and, after quoting the beautiful lines,

"Early to bed and early to rise. Make a man healthy, wealthy, and wise," he appoints each individual's task for the day, sets him at it with encouraging words, and goes back to bed again. [*Ba-dump-bump*] I mention here, in no fault-finding spirit, but with the deference justly due a man who is older and wiser and worthier than I, that he snores awfully. In a moment of irritation, once, I was rash enough to say I never would sleep with him until he broke himself of the unfortunate habit. I have kept my word with bigoted and unwavering determination.

At half-past eleven o'clock Mr. Greeley rises again. He shaves himself. He considers that there is great virtue and economy in shaving himself. He does it with a dull razor, [*Hinting perhaps that Mr. Greeley is cheap?*] sometimes humming a part of a tune (he knows part of a tune and takes an innocent delight in regarding it as the first half of Old Hundred; but parties familiar with that hymn have felt obliged to confess that they could not recognize it, and, therefore, the noise he makes is doubtless an unconscious original composition of Mr. Greeley's) and sometimes, when the razor is especially dull, he accompanies himself with a formula like this: "Damn the damned razor, and the damned outcast who made it."—H.G.

He then goes out into his model garden, and applies his vast store of agricultural knowledge to the amelioration of his cabbage: after which he writes an able agricultural article for the instruction of American farmers, his soul cheered the while with the reflection that if cabbages were worth eleven dollars apiece his model farm would pay.

He next goes to breakfast, which is a frugal, abstemious meal with him, [*cheap?*] and consists of nothing but just such things as the market affords, nothing more. He drinks nothing but water—nothing whatever but water and coffee, and tea, and Scotch ale, and lager beer and lemonade with a fly in it—sometimes a house fly, and sometimes a horse fly, according to the amount of inspiration required to warm him up to his daily duties. During breakfast he reads the Tribune all through, and enjoys the satisfaction of knowing that all the brilliant things in it, written by Young and Cooke and Hazard, and myself, [*this is his boss!*] are attributed to him by a confiding and infernal public. [*Infernal? A little jealousy, Mr. Twain?*]

After breakfast he writes a short editorial, and puts a large dash at the beginning of it, thus (-) which is the same as if he put H.G. after it, and takes a savage pleasure in reflecting that none of us understrappers can use that dash, except in profane conversation when chafing over the

Appendix B

outrage. [*Abuse of power?*] He writes this editorial in his own handwriting. He does it because he is so vain of his penmanship. He always did take an inordinate pride in his penmanship. He hired out once, in his young days, as a writing master, but the enterprise failed. The pupils could not translate his marks with any certainty. His first copy was "Virtue is its own reward," and they got it "Washing with soap is wholly absurd," and so the trustees discharged him for attempting to convey bad morals, through the medium of worse penmanship. [*Bad penmanship? An inside joke at* Tribune *offices?*] But, as I was saying, he writes his morning editorial. Then, he tries to read it over, and can't do it; and so they set it up at random, as you may say, putting in what words they can make out, and when they get aground on a long word they put in "reconstruction" or "universal suffrage" and spar off the paddle ahead, and next morning, if the degraded public can tell what it is all about, they say H.G. wrote it, and if they can't, they say it is one of those imbecile understrappers, and that is the end of it.

On Sundays Mr. Greeley sits in a prominent pew in Mr. Chaplin's church and lets on that he is asleep, and the congregation regard it as a eccentricity of genius. [*Zing!*]

When he is going to appear in public, Mr. Greeley spends two hours on his toilet. He is the most painstaking and elaborate man about getting up his dress that lives in America. This is his chiefest and pleasantest foible. He puts on a soiled shirt, saved from the wash, [*Cheap?*] and leaves one end of the collar unbuttoned. He puts on his most dilapidated hat, turns it wrong side before, cants it onto the back of his head, and jams and extra dent in the side of it. He puts on his most atrocious boots, [*Cheap?*] and spends fifteen minutes tucking the left leg of his pants into his boot top in what shall seem the most careless and unstudied way. But his cravat—it is into the arrangement of his cravat that he throws all his soul, all the powers of his great mind. After fixing at it for forty minutes before the glass it is perfect—it is askew in every way—[*A cheap slob?*] it overflows his coat-collar on one side and sinks into oblivion on the other—it climbs and delves around about his neck—the knot is conspicuously displayed under his left eye, and it stretches one of its long ends straight out horizontally, and the other goes after his eye, in the good old Toodles fashion—and then, completely and marvelously appareled, Mr. Greeley strides forth, rolling like a sailor, a miracle of astounding costumery, the awe and wonder of the nations! [*Sarcasm note!*]

But I haven't time to tell the rest of his private habits. Suffice it that he is an upright and honest man—a practical, great business man—a useful man to his nation and his generation—a famous man who has earned his celebrity—and withal the worst-dressed man in this or any other country, even though he does take so thundering much pains and put on so many frills about it.

Commentary

A lovely little introduction to Twain as a journalist. Teasing a famous journalist (more famous than Twain—then) in his own paper? His boss? Twain's irreverence here is priceless. What is he going to tell us about Horace Greeley that we don't already know?

"I mean his private habits. We know all about him as regards every other department of his life and service. Because, whenever a magazinist or a bookmaker is employed to write, and cannot think of a subject, he writes about Horace Greeley. Even the boys in the schools..."

We get it. Celebrity overload. And Twain is going to have more than a little fun with that, even if he's going to rag on the guy who published (and gave a great audience to) his letters from the Quaker City cruise to the Holy Land which comprised *Innocents Abroad*.

So he's about to bite the hand that literally fed him. And he's going to chomp down hard. Here, in a three-page nutshell, we have a great introduction to Twain's journalism; marked by sharp observation, irreverent humor and a compulsion, you might say, to go against the grain. The boys in school weren't writing about him, they were writing about Horace Greeley. He had to do something about that.

Questions for "The Private Habits of Horace Greeley"

(use complete sentences for every answer)

1. What do you think was Mark Twain's inspiration for this article?
2. Why, in your view, did Twain use the phrase—and dashes—"positively the last" in the opening of the story? Explain the effect on the reader.
3. Describe the tone of Twain's article.
4. What are the things that Twain "gets on" Greeley about?
5. At a time when "gossip" was rarely something you would find in

Appendix B

print, why, in your view, did Twain offer some—about his (sometime) boss?

6. Describe Twain's writing style in this article.
7. Why does Twain mention Greeley's "habit" of sleeping in church?
8. What does "amelioration" mean?
9. What does he mean by "a confiding and infernal public"?
10. What—in your view—was Twain's most insulting remark about Greeley?
11. Write a one-paragraph synopsis of Twain's article.
12. Write a one-paragraph analysis of Twain's article.

"An Encounter with an Interviewer" (1874)

Author's note: This piece was originally included in some of Twain's stage performances. If, as a teacher, you look forward to the opportunity to really surprise your students, to turn them upside down, this brief, almost Monty Python-esque piece is an imaginative way to do it. It's brief, funny, and almost crazy. And to perform it, I try and select a good reader, someone who is a serious student, to play the part of the interviewer and I read the Twain part, keeping in mind Hal Holbrook's mastery of the Mark Twain pause.

The premise is that the cub reporter gets a chance to interview the visiting writer on a book tour. And, as we quickly see from the questions, is no more prepared to query Mark Twain than he or she is to question Our Maker. What is fun about this is at first, my classes are almost always shocked at Twain's apparent rudeness to the interviewer. Their sympathies almost always are with the reporter. This is where, once you're done, you turn them on their head. So, let's look at Twain's "An Encounter with an Interviewer."

"An Encounter with an Interviewer" (Mark Twain)

The nervous, dapper, "peart" young man took the chair I offered him, and said he was connected with the *Daily Thunderstorm*, and added,—

(The Reporter) "Hoping it's no harm, I've come to interview you."

(Twain) "Come to what?"

"*Interview* you."

"Ah! I see. Yes,—yes. Um! Yes,—yes."

I was not feeling bright that morning. Indeed, my powers seemed a bit under a cloud. However, I went to the bookcase, and when I had been looking six or seven minutes, I found I was obliged to refer to the young man. I said,—

"How do you spell it?"

"Spell what?"

"Interview."

"O my goodness! What do you want to spell it for?"

"I don't want to spell it; I want to see what it means."

"Well, this is astonishing, I must say. *I* can tell you what it means, if you—if you—"

"O, all right! That will answer, and much obliged to you, too."

"I n, *in*, t e r, *ter*, *in*ter—"

"Then you spell it with an *I*?"

"Why, certainly!"

"O, that is what took me so long."

"Why, my *dear* sir, what did *you* propose to spell it with?"

"Well, I—I—I hardly know. I had the Unabridged, and I was ciphering around in the back end, hoping I might tree her among the pictures. But it's a very old edition."

"Why, my friend, they wouldn't have a *picture* of it in even the latest e— My dear sir, I beg your pardon, I mean no harm in the world, but you do not look as—as—intelligent as I had expected you would. No harm,—I mean no harm at all."

"O, don't mention it! It has often been said, and by people who would not flatter and who could have no inducement to flatter, that I am quite remarkable in that way. Yes,—yes; they always speak of it with rapture."

"I can easily imagine it. But about this interview. You know it is the custom, now, to interview any man who has become notorious."

"Indeed! I had not heard of it before. It must be very interesting. What do you do it with?"

"Ah, well,—well,—well,—this is disheartening. It *ought* to be done with a club in some cases; but customarily it consists in the interviewer asking questions and the interviewed answering them. It is all the rage now. Will you let me ask you certain questions calculated to bring out the salient points of your public and private history?"

"O, with pleasure,—with pleasure. I have a very bad memory, but I hope you will not mind that. That is to say, it is an irregular memory,—singularly

Appendix B

irregular. Sometimes it goes in a gallop, and then again it will be as much as a fortnight passing a given point. This is a great grief to me."

"O, it is no matter, so you will try to do the best you can."

"I will. I will put my whole mind on it."

"Thanks. Are you ready to begin?"

"Ready."

Q. How old are you?
   A. Nineteen, in June.

Q. Indeed! I would have taken you to be thirty-five or six. Where were you born?
   A. In Missouri.

Q. When did you begin to write?
   A. In 1836.

Q. Why, how could that be, if you are only nineteen now?
   A. I don't know. It does seem curious somehow.

Q. It does, indeed. Who do you consider the most remarkable man you ever met?
   A. Aaron Burr. *(On-stage, Holbrook usually substitutes George Washington, better audience recognition)*

Q. But you never could have met Aaron Burr, if you are only nineteen years—
   A. Now, if you know more about me than I do, what do you ask me for?

Q. Well, it was only a suggestion; nothing more. How did you happen to meet Burr?
   A. Well, I happened to be at his funeral one day, and he asked me to make less noise, and—

Q. But, good heavens! If you were at his funeral, he must have been dead; and if he was dead, how could he care whether you made a noise or not?
   A. I don't know. He was always a particular kind of a man that way.

Q. Still, I don't understand it at all. You say he spoke to you and that he was dead.
   A. I didn't say he was dead.

Selected Short Works by Twain, with Annotations

Q. But wasn't he dead?
　A. Well, some said he was, some said he wasn't.

Q. What do you think?
　A. O, it was none of my business! It wasn't any of my funeral.

Q. Did you— However, we can never get this matter straight. Let me ask about something else. What was the date of your birth?
　A. Monday, October 31, 1693.

Q. What! Impossible! That would make you a hundred and eighty years old. How do you account for that?
　A. I don't account for it at all.

Q. But you said at first you were only nineteen, and now you make yourself out to be one hundred and eighty. It is an awful discrepancy.
　A. Why, have you noticed that? (*Shaking hands.*) Many a time it has seemed to me like a discrepancy, but somehow I couldn't make up my mind. How quick you notice a thing!

Q. Thank you for the compliment, as far as it goes. Had you, or have you, any brothers or sisters?
　A. Eh! I—I—I think so,—yes,—but I don't remember.

Q. Well, that is the most extraordinary statement I ever heard!
　A. Why, what makes you think that?

Q. How could I think otherwise? Why, look here! who is this a picture of on the wall? Isn't that a brother of yours?
　A. Oh! yes, yes, yes! Now you remind me of it, that *was* a brother of mine. That's William,—*Bill* we called him. Poor old Bill!

Q. Why? Is he dead, then?
　A. Ah, well, I suppose so. We never could tell. There was a great mystery about it.

Q. That is sad, very sad. He disappeared, then?
　A. Well, yes, in a sort of general way. We buried him.

Q. Buried him! Buried him without knowing whether he was dead or not?
　A. O no! Not that. He was dead enough.

Appendix B

Q. Well, I confess that I can't understand this. If you buried him and you knew he was dead—
A. No! no! we only thought he was.

Q. O, I see! He came to life again?
A. I bet he didn't.

Q. Well, I never heard anything like this. Somebody was dead. Somebody was buried. Now, where was the mystery?
A. Ah, that's just it! That's it exactly. You see we were twins,—defunct and I,—and we got mixed in the bath-tub when we were only two weeks old, and one of us was drowned. But we didn't know which. Some think it was Bill, some think it was me.

Q. Well, that is remarkable. What do you think?
A. Goodness knows! I would give whole worlds to know. This solemn, this awful mystery has cast a gloom over my whole life. But I will tell you a secret now, which I never have revealed to any creature before. One of us had a peculiar mark, a large mole on the back of the left hand,—that was *me*. That child was the one that was drowned.

Q. Very well, then, I don't see that there is any mystery about it, after all.
A. You don't? Well, *I* do. Anyway I don't see how they could ever have been such a blundering lot as to go and bury the wrong child. But, 'sh!— don't mention it where the family can hear of it. Heaven knows they have heart-breaking troubles enough without adding this.

Q. Well, I believe I have got material enough for the present, and I am very much obliged to you for the pains you have taken. But I was a good deal interested in that account of Aaron Burr's funeral. Would you mind telling me what particular circumstance it was that made you think Burr was such a remarkable man?
A. O, it was a mere trifle! Not one man in fifty would have noticed it at all. When the sermon was over, and the procession all ready to start for the cemetery, and the body all arranged nice in the hearse, he said he wanted to take a last look at the scenery, and so he *got up and rode with the driver.*

Then the young man reverently withdrew. He was very pleasant company, and I was sorry to see him go.

Selected Short Works by Twain, with Annotations

Commentary

At this point, the students usually have a puzzled look on their face. They know about Mark Twain, they like him and are, flatly, surprised he's treated this reporter so rudely. It's then you get to explain that what Twain really did in that very strange interview, it was a gift. I explain it this way: the cub reporter probably also had to cover a fire, a ballet recital, the opening of a new business and who knows what else? Very clearly, the reporter is not the least bit prepared or knowledgeable about his subject. After a bit of an intentionally stumbling start—we are anxious for him to get on with the interview—he begins with a twinkle in his eye.

By 1874, Twain was 39 years old but, as we'll see, even that was worth playing with. The reporter begins with a question that an experienced reporter would never ask but already know: "How old are you?" This tips off Twain that his interviewer is not too sharp. So Twain gives a nifty retort: "Nineteen, in June." Laughs all around. Make sure you put that pause in after "Nineteen." And then, "in June." Funny stuff.

The reporter tries to keep things moving, asking two more questions a reporter shouldn't have to—where were you born and when did you begin to write? Twain's straight-faced quip: "1836 (actually a year after his birth)" And the reporter's dim-witted question? "Why, how could that be, if you are only nineteen now?" And Twain gives the response that every interviewee would likely to offer—"I don't know. It does seem curious somehow."

It's right here that we can see who is really controlling this interview—and the fun he's having doing it. This is where you show your class that the ultimate result of what he's done is the reporter goes back to the newspaper, to his or her editor and say, "You would not believe what that Twain guy said..." So instead of writing what would be an incredibly tedious story if he just answered the questions—"Where were you born? When did you first begin to write?"—the reporter has a story, one that will definitely be read.

On stage, Holbrook has used this "Encounter with an Interviewer" piece, editing it just a little bit. And he made one interesting edit, changing Aaron Burr (who Twain said was the most remarkable man he ever met) to George Washington, someone everyone knows. It's an excellent change and one that leads us through the absurdities that close out the story: Burr/Washington sitting up and asking him to make less noise, then Twain wondering about his long, lost twin, the one that drowned in the bathtub.

Appendix B

Some Questions for Your Students

1. Why, in your view, didn't Twain simply tell the reporter, the questions you're asking are lousy?
2. How surprised were you by Twain's responses?
3. How do you think the reporter presented the interview to his/her editor?
4. Why does this article still make us laugh?
5. If Mark Twain were around today, would he be a writer or a TV host?

"A Presidential Candidate": Twain's Satirical Look at Campaigns and Candidates

Author's note: By 1879, Mark Twain was recognized across the world as a humorist and successful American writer. He'd written Innocents Abroad *and most recently,* The Adventures of Tom Sawyer *and many popular magazine articles and stories made him a celebrated man of letters. When he turned his gaze at the messy Presidential race of 1880, he kept a close eye on the newspapers of the day and had a humorous—and as we look at it now, prescient—take on the entire electoral process and how the media impacts the presidential race, justly or not.*

President Rutherford B. Hayes, who was not likely to be re-elected anyway, had announced he was not going to run for a second term. Former President Ulysses S. Grant, a close Twain friend (Twain would help Grant publish his memoirs a few years later) had decided that, since there didn't seem to be any other popular candidates, he would try to run for a third term. Though Grant had a scandal-ridden eight years in the White House and left office under a cloud, the country was reeling and skeptical of all politicians anyway. So, Grant thought he'd give it one more try. Though Grant was the leading candidate on the first ballot, he didn't have enough support to be nominated. Some 34 ballots later, the Republican Party nominated an experienced but not particularly well-known figure, James A. Garfield, who won the election, served for four months and was shot and killed by a deranged assassin.

Twain didn't know all that was going to happen, but he did have a sense that where the American Presidency was headed was not what the Founding Fathers had in mind. The article "A Presidential Candidate" ran in the New York Evening Post *on June 9, 1879,*

Selected Short Works by Twain, with Annotations

just about a year before the Republican Convention in Chicago. As you read it, think of all the themes that Twain jokingly touched on that have come up in the intervening campaigns.

"A Presidential Candidate"

By Mark Twain
New York Evening Post (June 9, 1879).

I have pretty much made up my mind to run for President. What the country wants is a candidate who cannot be injured by investigation of his past history, so that the enemies of the party will be unable to rake up anything against him that nobody ever heard of before. If you know the worst about a candidate, to begin with, every attempt to spring things on him will be checkmated. [*Twain's point about elections still rings true; what can you dig up on your opposition? Like Donald Trump, Jr.'s meeting with the Russians in 2016.*]

Now I am going to enter the field with an open record. I am going to own up in advance to all the wickedness I have done, and if any Congressional committee is disposed to prowl around my biography in the hope of discovering any dark and deadly deed that I have secreted, why—let it prowl.

In the first place, I admit that I treed a rheumatic grandfather of mine in the winter of 1850. He was old and inexpert in climbing trees, but with the heartless brutality that is characteristic of me I ran him out of the front door in his nightshirt at the point of a shotgun, and caused him to bowl up a maple tree, where he remained all night, while I emptied shot into his legs. I did this because he snored. I will do it again if I ever have another grandfather. I am as inhuman now as I was in 1850. [*Wouldn't it be amazing if candidates were this frank?*]

I candidly acknowledge that I ran away at the battle of Gettysburg. My friends have tried to smooth over this fact by asserting that I did so for the purpose of imitating Washington, who went into the woods at Valley Forge for the purpose of saying his prayers. [*I always have to explain this historical allusion to my classes. Not much background knowledge of George Washington.*] It was a miserable subterfuge. I struck out in a straight line for the Tropic of Cancer because I was scared. I wanted my country saved, but I preferred to have somebody else save it. [*Again, Twain says precisely the opposite of what we expect*] I entertain that preference

117

Appendix B

yet. If the bubble reputation can be obtained only at the cannon's mouth, I am willing to go there for it, provided the cannon is empty. If it is loaded my immortal and inflexible purpose is to get over the fence and go home. My invariable practice in war has been to bring out of every fight two-thirds more men than when I went in. This seems to me to be Napoleonic in its grandeur. [*Another apt historical reference that needs explanation.*]

My financial views are of the most decided character, but they are not likely, perhaps, to increase my popularity with the advocates of inflation. I do not insist upon the special supremacy of rag money or hard money. The great fundamental principle of my life is to take any kind I can get. [*This is still applicable, isn't it?*]

The rumor that I buried a dead aunt under my grapevine was correct. The vine needed fertilizing, my aunt had to be buried, and I dedicated her to this high purpose. Does that unfit me for the Presidency? The Constitution of our country does not say so. [*Parsing the language of the Constitution ahead of Presidents*] No other citizen was ever considered unworthy of this office because he enriched his grapevines with his dead relatives. Why should I be selected as the victim of an absurd prejudice.

I admit also that I am not a friend of the poor man. I regard the poor man, in his present condition, as so much wasted raw material. Cut up and properly canned, he might be made useful to fatten the natives of the cannibal islands and improve our export trade with that region. [*Whaaaaat?*] I shall recommend legislation upon the subject in my first message. My campaign cry will be: "Desiccate the poor workingman; stuff him into sausages." [*Desiccate? Oh my.*]

These are about the worst parts of my record. On them I come before the country. If my country don't want me, I will go back again. But I recommend myself as a safe man—a man who starts from the basis of total depravity and proposes to be fiendish to the last.

Commentary

Ahead of the curve, Twain suggests that it's not about a man's qualifications, God forbid, it's about what they can nail him on. Think Clinton's philandering, Nixon's dog, Carter's "lust in his heart," Romney's dog, Dukakis' paroles, etc. It was never—and evidently WILL never be—about who SHOULD be president, or who would make a good president. It's all about who would be a bad one because ... "Now I am going to enter the field with an open record," he writes. "I am going to own up in advance to all the wickedness I have done, and if any Congressional committee is disposed to prowl around my biography in the hope of discovering any dark and deadly deed that I have secreted, why—let it prowl."

So ... what did he do? Twain rattles off a comical sequence of misdeeds: forcing a rheumatic grandfather up a tree, shooting him in the legs with birdshot because he snored, that he was a coward at Gettysburg and deserted because he was scared. Imagine a candidate offering that thunderbolt of honesty!

And he followed that up with a line that could have applied to many a recent candidate: "I wanted my country," Twain writes, "but I wanted someone else to save it." A candidate who's brutal, heartless, a coward ... what else can Twain share?

Certainly, he wrote this to be humorous, and it is. But isn't it just a little too close the bone in some spots? You could run this article in the daily newspaper and people would say, "Gee, elections haven't changed much, have they?"

Some Questions for Your Students

1. "Running for President" is a good example of satire. How do we know it's satire?
2. In your view, what is Twain's most convincing point?
3. Judging from this article, what do you think Twain's opinion of politicians is?
4. Why does this article still seem applicable to today's politicians and current elections?
5. If you were a candidate, what would be the worst thing they could say about you?

"How I Edited an Agricultural Paper (Once)" (1870)

Author's note: GOALS—Introduce Twain and his use of exaggeration and his sense that his audience knows at least a little bit about farming. And vegetables.

Appendix B

"How I Edited an Agricultural Paper (Once)" (Mark Twain)

I did not take temporary [*Notice he tips us off right away that it was TEMPORARY*] editorship of an agricultural paper without misgivings. Neither would a landsman take command of a ship without misgivings. [*Hint*] But I was in circumstances that made the salary an object. [*He's broke*] The regular editor of the paper was going off for a holiday, and I accepted the terms he offered, and took his place.

The sensation of being at work again was luxurious, and I wrought all the week with unflagging pleasure. We went to press, and I waited a day with some solicitude to see whether my effort was going to attract any notice. As I left the office, toward sundown, a group of men and boys at the foot of the stairs dispersed with one impulse, and gave me passageway, and I heard one or two of them say: "That's him!" [*Good example here of a unreliable narrator. We suspect they're pointing him out for other reasons.*]

I was naturally pleased by this incident. The next morning I found a similar group at the foot of the stairs, and scattering couples and individuals standing here and there in the street, and over the way, watching me with interest. The group separated and fell back as I approached, and I heard a man say, "Look at his eye!" I pretended not to observe the notice I was attracting, but secretly I was pleased with it, and was purposing to write an account of it to my aunt. [*Again, he doesn't get it—we do.*]

I went up the short flight of stairs, and heard cheery voices and a ringing laugh as I drew near the door, which I opened, and caught a glimpse of two young rural-looking men, whose faces blanched and lengthened when they saw me, and then they both plunged through the window with a great crash. I was surprised. (Comic response.)

In about half an hour an old gentleman, with a flowing beard and a fine but rather austere face, entered, and sat down at my invitation. He seemed to have something on his mind. He took off his hat and set it on the floor, and got out of it a red silk handkerchief and a copy of our paper.

He put the paper on his lap, and while he polished his spectacles with his handkerchief, he said, "Are you the new editor?"

I said I was.

"Have you ever edited an agricultural paper before?"

Selected Short Works by Twain, with Annotations

"No," I said; "this is my first attempt."

"Very likely. Have you had any experience in agriculture practically?"

"No. I believe I have not."

"Some instinct told me so," said the old gentleman, putting on his spectacles, and looking over them at me with asperity, while he folded his paper into a convenient shape. "I wish to read you what must have made me have that instinct. It was this editorial. [*Finally, we get to hear what all the fuss is about.*] Listen, and see if it was you that wrote it: 'Turnips should never be pulled, it injures them. It is much better to send a boy up and let him shake the tree.'"

"Now, what do you think of that?—for I really suppose you wrote it?"

"Think of it? Why, I think it is good. I think it is sense. I have no doubt that every year millions and millions of bushels of turnips are spoiled in this township alone by being pulled in a half-ripe condition, when, if they had sent a boy up to shake the tree..."

"Shake your grandmother! Turnips don't grow on trees!"

"Oh, they don't, don't they? Well, who said they did? The language was intended to be figurative, wholly figurative. Anybody that knows anything will know that I meant that the boy should shake the vine."

[*This assumes, of course, that the reader fully understands that turnips don't grow on trees or on a vine. Even if you don't know agriculture, you get it from the way he says it.*]

Then this old person got up and tore his paper all into small shreds, and stamped on them, and broke several things with his cane, and said I did not know as much as a cow; and then went out and banged the door after him, and, in short, acted in such a way that *I fancied he was displeased about something. But not knowing what the trouble was, I could not be any help to him.* [*This is about what Stan Laurel might have said in similar circumstances. He doesn't get it.*]

Pretty soon after this a long cadaverous creature, with lanky locks hanging down to his shoulders, and a week's stubble bristling from the hills and valleys of his face, darted within the door, and halted, motionless, with finger on lip, and head and body bent in listening attitude. No sound was heard. Still he listened. No sound. Then he turned the key in the door, and came elaborately tiptoeing toward me till he was within long reaching distance of me, when he stopped, and after scanning my face with intense interest for a while, drew a folded copy of our paper from his bosom, and said:

"There, you wrote that. Read it to me, quick! Relieve me. I suffer."

Appendix B

I read as follows; and as the sentences fell from my lips I could see the relief come, I could see the drawn muscles relax, and the anxiety go out of the face, and rest and peace steal over the features like the merciful moonlight over a desolate landscape [*lovely bit of exaggeration here—to comic effect*]:

"The guano [*Guano is another name for bird poop*] is a fine bird, but great care is necessary in rearing it. It should not be imported earlier than June or later than September. In the winter it should be kept in a warm place, where it can hatch out its young.

"It is evident that we are to have a backward season for grain. Therefore it will be well for the farmer to begin setting out his cornstalks and planting his buckwheat cakes in July instead of August.

"Concerning the pumpkin. This berry is a favorite with the natives of the interior of New England, who prefer it to the goose-berry for the making of fruit-cake, and who likewise give it the preference over the raspberry for feeding cows, as being more filling and fully as satisfying. The pumpkin is the only esculent of the orange family that will thrive in the North, except the gourd and one or two varieties of the squash. But the custom of planting it in the front yard with the shrubbery is fast going out of vogue, for it is now generally conceded that the pumpkin as a shade tree is a failure.

"Now, as the warm weather approaches, and the ganders begin to spawn..."

The excited listener sprang toward me to shake hands, and said, "There, there, that will do. I know I am all right now, because you have read it just as I did, word for word. But, stranger, when I first read it this morning, I said to myself, I never, never believed it before, notwithstanding my friends kept me under watch so strict, but now I believe I am crazy; and with that I fetched a howl that you might have heard two miles, and started out to kill somebody—because, you know, I knew it would come to that sooner or later, and so I might as well begin. I read one of them paragraphs over again, so as to be certain, and then I burned my house down and started. I have crippled several people, and have got one fellow up a tree, where I can get him if I want him. But I thought I would call in here as I passed along and make the thing perfectly certain; and now it is certain, and I tell you it is lucky for the chap that is in the tree. I should have killed him, sure, as I went back. Goodbye, sir, good-bye; you have taken a great load off my mind. My reason has stood the strain of one of your agricultural articles, and I know that nothing can ever unseat it now. Good-bye, sir."

Selected Short Works by Twain, with Annotations

I felt a little uncomfortable about the cripplings and arsons this person had been entertaining himself with, for I could not help feeling remotely accessory to them. [*Again, he doesn't get it. We do.*] But these thoughts were quickly banished, for the regular editor walked in! [I thought to myself, now if you had gone to Egypt as I recommended you to, I might have had a chance to get my hand in; but you wouldn't do it, and here you are. I sort of expected you.]

The editor was looking sad and perplexed and dejected.

He surveyed the wreck, which that old rioter and these two young farmers had made, and then said, "This is a sad business—a very sad business. There is the mucilage-bottle broken, and six panes of glass, and a spittoon and two candlesticks. But that is not the worst. The reputation of the paper is injured—and permanently, I fear. *True, there never was such a call for the paper before, and it never sold such a large edition or soared to such celebrity; but does one want to be famous for lunacy, and prosper upon the infirmities of his mind?*

[*While this is a comic piece, does Twain, unwittingly, prepare us for the tabloids, with their stories about Elvis coming back, two-headed babies, aliens sliding into second, and so forth? Do you want to be famous for lunacy? Just plain famous? Just sell papers? It's not as far-fetched an idea as it seems.*]

My friend, as I am an honest man, the street out here is full of people, and others are roosting on the fences, waiting to get a glimpse of you, because they think you crazy. And well they might after reading your editorials. They are a disgrace to journalism. Why, what put it into your head that you could edit a paper of this nature? You do not seem to know the first rudiments of agriculture. You speak of a furrow and a harrow as being the same thing; you talk of the moulting season for cows; and you recommend the domestication of the pole-cat on account of its playfulness and its excellence as a ratter! Your remark that clams will lie quiet if music be played to them was superfluous—entirely superfluous. Nothing disturbs clams. Clams always lie quiet. Clams care nothing whatever about music.

Ah, heavens and earth, friend! If you had made the acquiring of ignorance the study of your life, you could not have graduated with higher honor than you could to-day. I never saw anything like it. Your observation that the horse chestnut as an article of commerce is steadily gaining in favor is simply calculated to destroy this journal. I want you to throw up your situation and go. I want no more holiday—I could not enjoy it if I

Appendix B

had it. Certainly not with you in my chair. I would always stand in dread of what you might be going to recommend next. It makes me lose all patience every time I think of your discussing oyster-beds under the head of 'Landscape Gardening.' I want you to go. Nothing on earth could persuade me to take another holiday. Oh! why didn't you tell me you didn't know anything about agriculture?"

[*The editor has had his say and it's a good one, explaining, logically, why what his new "editor" did was so wrong. This is what the reader expects the real editor to say and Twain, of course, knows this. But he has his counterargument ready.*]

"Tell you, you cornstalk, you cabbage, you son of a cauliflower? It's the first time I ever heard such an unfeeling remark. I tell you I have been in the editorial business going on 14 years, and it is the first time I ever heard of a man's having to know anything in order to edit a newspaper. You turnip! Who write the dramatic critiques for the second-rate papers? Why, a parcel of promoted shoemakers and apprentice apothecaries, who know just as much about good acting as I do about good farming and no more. *[Ah! We see where Twain got the idea!]* Who review the books? People who never wrote one. Who do up the heavy leaders on finance? Parties who have had the largest opportunities for knowing nothing about it. Who criticize the Indian campaigns? Gentlemen who do not know a war-whoop from a wigwam, and who never have had to run a foot race with a tomahawk, or pluck arrows out of the several members of their families to build the evening camp-fire with. Who write the temperance appeals, and clamor about the flowing bowl? Folks who will never draw another sober breath till they do it in the grave. Who edit the agricultural papers, you—yam? Men, as a general thing, who fail in the poetry line, yellow covered novel line, sensation-drama line, city-editor line, and finally fall back on agriculture as a temporary reprieve from the poorhouse. You try to tell me anything about the newspaper business!

Sir, I have been through it from Alpha to Omaha, and I tell you that the less a man knows the bigger the noise he makes and the higher the salary he commands. Heaven knows if I had been ignorant instead of cultivated, and impudent instead of diffident, I could have made a name for myself in this cold selfish world. I take my leave, sir. Since I have been treated as you have treated me, I am perfectly willing to go. But I have done my duty. I have fulfilled my contract as far as I was permitted to do it. I said I could make your paper of interest to all classes—and I have. I

Selected Short Works by Twain, with Annotations

said I could run your circulation up to 20,000 copies, and if I had had two more weeks I'd have done it. And I'd have given you the best class of readers that ever an agricultural paper had—not a farmer in it, nor a solitary individual who could tell a watermelon tree from a peach vine to save his life. You are the loser by this rupture, not me, Pie-plant. Adios."

I then left.

[*Funny stuff. This is instructive for readers to see where, sometimes hidden in the middle of a work, you see where an author gets an idea. It's also educational to see how Twain sets up the two confrontations before the real editor gets back, sets up our expectations for a lecture, delivers and then leaves us with a delightful twist.*]

"An Entertaining Article": Twain's Classic Literary Prank

Author's note: This is a personal favorite. I had never heard or or read this article until a few years ago. It's somewhat of a mystery in Twainlore, as I've never read him comment on it or seen much critical reaction to it. To me, it's a scream. Who but Mark Twain would think of reviewing his own book—and PANNING it?

By 1870, Mark Twain was just beginning to reap the benefits of celebrity and literary achievements. His collections of newspaper letters from his trip to Europe and the Holy Land had been combined into his unique travelogue, Innocents Abroad, *and Twain's lively account of his trip was a success. He was starting to make his way as a prominent American writer.*

So when Innocents *started to draw reviews in prominent places, like in* The Atlantic *by William Dean Howells, no less, Twain decided to have a little fun with the whole process.*

Since his irreverent look at Europe and the Holy Land was certain to draw some criticism, Twain thought he'd get ahead of the curve, so to speak, by offering his own critique. Posing as a British literary critic, Twain wrote his own scathing and delightfully playful assessment of his very own book. This is the way Mark Twain thought. "An Entertaining Article" is the result.

"An Entertaining Article" (Mark Twain)

I take the following paragraph from an article in the *Boston Advertiser*:

Appendix B

"Perhaps the most successful flights of the humor of Mark Twain have been descriptions of the persons who did not appreciate his humor at all. We have become familiar with the Californians who were thrilled with terror by his burlesque of a newspaper reporter's way of telling a story, and we have heard of the Pennsylvania clergyman who sadly returned his *Innocents Abroad* to the book-agent with the remark that 'the man who could shed tears over the tomb of Adam must be an idiot.' But Mark Twain may now add a much more glorious instance to his string of trophies. The *Saturday Review*, in its number of October 8th, reviews his book of travels, which has been republished in England, and reviews it seriously. We can imagine the delight of the humorist in reading this tribute to his power; and indeed it is so amusing in itself that he can hardly do better than reproduce the article in full in his next monthly Memoranda."

(Publishing the above paragraph thus, gives me a sort of authority for reproducing the *Saturday Review*'s article in full in these pages. I dearly wanted to do it, for I cannot write anything half so delicious myself. If I had a cast-iron dog that could read this English criticism and preserve his austerity, I would drive him off the door-step.)

(From the London "*Saturday Review*.")

[*Note: Remind your class—THIS IS TWAIN WRITING, pretending to be a book reviewer!*]

"Reviews of New Books"

"*The Innocents Abroad. A Book of Travels.* By Mark Twain. London: Hotten, publisher. 1870. "Lord Macaulay died too soon. We never felt this so deeply as when we finished the last chapter of the above- named extravagant work. Macaulay died too soon—for none but he could mete out complete and comprehensive justice to the insolence, the impertinence, the presumption, the mendacity, and, above all, the majestic ignorance of this author. [*Now that's an opening sentence for you; the insolence, the impertinence, the presumption, the mendacity, the majestic ignorance...*]

"To say that the *Innocents Abroad* is a curious book, would be to use the faintest language—would be to speak of the Matterhorn as a neat elevation or of Niagara as being 'nice' or 'pretty.' 'Curious' is too tame a word wherewith to describe the imposing insanity of this work. There is no word that is large enough or long enough. Let us, therefore, photograph a passing glimpse of book and author, and trust the rest to the reader. Let the cultivated English student of human nature picture to himself this Mark Twain as a person capable of doing the following-described things—

and not only doing them, but with incredible innocence printing them calmly and tranquilly in a book. [*Twain, 'incredibly innocent? Do tell...*]
For instance:

"He states that he entered a hair-dresser's in Paris to get shaved, and the first 'rake' the barber gave with his razor it loosened his 'hide' and lifted him out of the chair. [*And so here begins a razor sharp recounting of Twain's classic exaggerative style of writing, perhaps aimed at humorless editors who just did not get his humor, like this reviewer.*]

"This is unquestionably exaggerated. In Florence he was so annoyed by beggars that he pretends to have seized and eaten one in a frantic spirit of revenge. There is, of course, no truth in this. He gives at full length a theatrical programme seventeen or eighteen hundred years old, which he professes to have found in the ruins of the Coliseum, among the dirt and mould and rubbish. It is a sufficient comment upon this statement to remark that even a cast-iron programme would not have lasted so long under such circumstances. In Greece he plainly betrays both fright and flight upon one occasion, but with frozen effrontery puts the latter in this falsely tame form: 'We sidled towards the Piræus.' 'Sidled,' indeed! He does not hesitate to intimate that at Ephesus, when his mule strayed from the proper course, he got down, took him under his arm, carried him to the road again, pointed him right, remounted, and went to sleep contentedly till it was time to restore the beast to the path once more. He states that a growing youth among his ship's passengers was in the constant habit of appeasing his hunger with soap and oakum between meals. In Palestine he tells of ants that came eleven miles to spend the summer in the desert and brought their provisions with them; yet he shows by his description of the country that the feat was an impossibility. He mentions, as if it were the most commonplace of matters, that he cut a Moslem in two in broad daylight in Jerusalem, with Godfrey de Bouillon's sword, and would have shed more blood if he had had a graveyard of his own. These statements are unworthy a moment's attention. Mr. Twain or any other foreigner who did such a thing in Jerusalem would be mobbed, and would infallibly lose his life. But why go on? Why repeat more of his audacious and exasperating falsehoods? Let us close fittingly with this one: he affirms that 'in the mosque of St. Sophia at Constantinople I got my feet so stuck up with a complication of gums, slime, and general impurity, that I wore out more than two thousand pair of bootjacks getting my boots off that night, and even then some Christian hide peeled off with them.'

Appendix B

[*By this point, if you're not laughing, perhaps you're an editor. How delightful that Twain was able to do that with his own writing. What a talent!*] It is monstrous. Such statements are simply lies—there is no other name for them. Will the reader longer marvel at the brutal ignorance that pervades the American nation when we tell him that we are informed upon perfectly good authority that this extravagant compilation of falsehoods, this exhaustless mine of stupendous lies, this *Innocents Abroad*, has actually been adopted by the schools and colleges of several of the States as a text-book! [*A textbook! The blasphemy of it all. Twain must have enjoyed writing this article as much as anything he ever did.*]

"But if his falsehoods are distressing, his innocence and his ignorance are enough to make one burn the book and despise the author. In one place he was so appalled at the sudden spectacle of a murdered man, unveiled by the moonlight, that he jumped out of the window, going through sash and all, and then remarks with the most childlike simplicity that he 'was not scared, but was considerably agitated.' It puts us out of patience to note that the simpleton is densely unconscious that Lucrezia Borgia ever existed off the stage. He is vulgarly ignorant of all foreign languages, but is frank enough to criticise the Italians' use of their own tongue. He says they spell the name of their great painter 'Vinci, but pronounce it Vinchy'—and then adds with a naïveté possible only to helpless ignorance, 'foreigners always spell better than they pronounce.' In another place he commits the bald absurdity of putting the phrase 'tare an ouns' into an Italian's mouth. In Rome he unhesitatingly believes the legend that St. Philip Neri's heart was so inflamed with divine love that it burst his ribs—believes it wholly because an author with a learned list of university degrees strung after his name endorses it—'otherwise,' says this gentle idiot, 'I should have felt a curiosity to know what Philip had for dinner.' [*Gentle idiot, indeed. It must have been difficult for him to stop, once he started picking his own writing apart with such inordinate glee.*]

Our author makes a long, fatiguing journey to the Grotto del Cane on purpose to test its poisoning powers on a dog—got elaborately ready for the experiment, and then discovered that he had no dog. A wiser person would have kept such a thing discreetly to himself, but with this harmless creature everything comes out. He hurts his foot in a rut two thousand years old in exhumed Pompeii, and presently, when staring at one of the cinder-like corpses unearthed in the next square, conceives the idea that may be it is the remains of the ancient Street Commissioner, [*How could anyone read that and not laugh? How could any book reviewer not get it?*] and straightway his horror softens down to a sort of chirpy contentment with the condition of things. In Damascus he visits the well of Ananias, three thousand years old, and is as surprised and delighted as a child to find that the water is 'as pure and fresh as if the well had been dug yesterday.' In the Holy Land he gags desperately at the hard Arabic and Hebrew Biblical names, and finally concludes to call them Baldwinsville, Williamsburgh, and so on, 'for convenience of spelling.'

"We have thus spoken freely of this man's stupefying simplicity and innocence, but we cannot deal similarly with his colossal ignorance. We do not know where to begin. And if we knew where to begin, we certainly would not know where to leave off. We will give one specimen, and one only. He did not know, until he got to Rome, that Michael Angelo was dead! And then, instead of crawling away and hiding his shameful ignorance somewhere, he proceeds to express a pious, grateful sort of satisfaction that he is gone and out of his troubles!

"No, the reader may seek out the author's exhibition of his uncultivation for himself. The book is absolutely dangerous, considering the magnitude and variety of its misstatements, and the convincing confidence with which they are made. And yet it is a text-book in the schools of America. [*A text book? Really? And the reviewer didn't question it?*]

The poor blunderer mouses among the sublime creations of the Old Masters, trying to acquire the elegant proficiency in art-knowledge, which he has a groping sort of comprehension is a proper thing for the travelled man to be able to display. But what is the manner of his study? And what is the progress he achieves? To what extent does he familiarize himself with the great pictures of Italy, and what degree of appreciation does he arrive at? Read:

"'When we see a monk going about with a lion and looking up into heaven, we know that that is St. Mark. When we see a monk with a book and a pen, looking tranquilly up to heaven, trying to think of a word, we know that that is St. Matthew. When we see a monk sitting on a rock, looking tranquilly up to heaven, with a human skull beside him, and without other baggage, we know that that is St. Jerome. Because we know that he always went flying light in the matter of baggage. When we see other monks looking tranquilly up to heaven, but having no trade-mark, we always ask who those parties are. We do this because we humbly wish to learn.'

Appendix B

"He then enumerates the thousands and thousands of copies of these several pictures which he has seen, and adds with accustomed simplicity that he feels encouraged to believe that when he has seen 'Some More' of each, and had a larger experience, he will eventually 'begin to take an absorbing interest in them'—the vulgar boor.

"That we have shown this to be a remarkable book, we think no one will deny. That it is a pernicious book to place in the hands of the confiding and uninformed, we think we have also shown. That the book is a deliberate and wicked creation of a diseased mind, is apparent upon every page. Having placed our judgement thus upon record, let us close with what charity we can, by remarking that even in this volume there is some good to be found; for whenever the author talks of his own country and lets Europe alone, he never fails to make himself interesting, and not only interesting, but instructive. No one can read without benefit his occasional chapters and paragraphs, about life in the gold and silver mines of California and Nevada; about the Indians of the plains and deserts of the West, and their cannibalism; about the raising of vegetables in kegs of gunpowder by the aid of two or three teaspoonfuls of guano; [*Not only is Guano a funny word, it is poop*] about the moving of small farms from place to place at night in wheelbarrows to avoid taxes; and about a sort of cows and mules in the Humboldt mines, that climb down chimneys and disturb the people at night. These matters are not only new, but are well worth knowing. It is a pity the author did not put in more of the same kind. His book is well written and is exceedingly entertaining, and so it just barely escaped being quite valuable also."

(One month later)

[*Now that the "review" has been published and drawn a response, Twain is reacting to the reaction to "his" review*]

Latterly I have received several letters, and see a number of newspaper paragraphs, all upon a certain subject, and all of about the same tenor. I here give honest specimens. One is from a New York paper, one is from a letter from an old friend, and one is from a letter from a New York publisher who is a stranger to me. I humbly endeavor to make these bits tooth-some with the remark that the article they are praising (which appeared in the December *Galaxy*, and pretended to be a criticism from the *London Saturday Review* on my *Innocents Abroad*) was written by myself, every line of it:

"*The Herald* says the richest thing out is the 'serious critique' in the *London Saturday Review*, on Mark Twain's *Innocents Abroad*. We thought before we read it that it must be 'serious,' as everybody said so, and were even ready to shed a few tears; but since perusing it, we are bound to confess that next to Mark Twain's 'Jumping Frog' it's the finest bit of humor and sarcasm that we've come across in many a day."

(I do not get a compliment like that every day.)

"I used to think that your writings were pretty good, but after reading the criticism in *The Galaxy* from the *London Review*, have discovered what an ass I must have been. If suggestions are in order, mine is, that you put that article in your next edition of the Innocents, as an extra chapter, if you are not afraid to put your own humor in competition with it. It is as rich a thing as I ever read."

(Which is a strong commendation from a book publisher.)

"*The London Reviewer*, my friend, is not the stupid, 'serious' creature he pretends to be, I think; but, on the contrary, has a keen appreciation and enjoyment of your book. As I read his article in *The Galaxy*, I could imagine him giving vent to many a hearty laugh. But he is writing for Catholics and Established Church people, and high-toned, antiquated, conservative gentility, whom it is a delight to him to help you shock, while he pretends to shake his head with owlish density. He is a magnificent humorist himself." (Now that is graceful and handsome. I take off my hat to my lifelong friend and comrade, and with my feet together and my fingers spread over my heart, I say, in the language of Alabama, "You do me proud.")

I stand guilty of the authorship of the article, but I did not mean any harm. I saw by an item in the *Boston Advertiser* that a solemn, serious critique on the English edition of my book had appeared in the *London Saturday Review*, and the idea of such a literary breakfast by a stolid, ponderous British ogre of the quill was too much for a naturally weak virtue, and I went home and burlesqued it—reveled in it, I may say. I never saw a copy of the real *Saturday Review* criticism until after my burlesque was written and mailed to the printer. But when I did get hold of a copy, I found it to be vulgar, awkwardly written, ill- natured, and entirely serious and in earnest. The gentleman who wrote the newspaper paragraph above quoted had not been misled as to its character. [*In other words, even after Twain came out and admitted he'd written the "review" people didn't believe him. Which made it even funnier. To Twain and us.*]

If any man doubts my word now, I will kill him. No, I will not kill him; I will win his money. I will bet him twenty to one, and let any New York publisher hold the stakes, that the statements I have above made as

Appendix B

to the authorship of the article in question are entirely true. Perhaps I may get wealthy at this, for I am willing to take all the bets that offer; and if a man wants larger odds, I will give him all he requires. But he ought to find out whether I am betting on what is termed "a sure thing" or not before he ventures his money, and he can do that by going to a public library and examining the *London Saturday Review* of October 8th, which contains the real critique.

Bless me, some people thought that I was the "sold" person!

P. S.—I cannot resist the temptation to toss in this most savory thing of all—this easy, graceful, philosophical disquisition, with its happy, chirping confidence. It is from the *Cincinnati Enquirer*: [*People still aren't buying that Twain wrote it. Nothing could please him more. Imagine if he lived in a time of tweets and social media.*]

"Nothing is more uncertain than the value of a fine cigar. Nine smokers out of ten would prefer an ordinary domestic article, three for a quarter, to a fifty-cent Partaga, if kept in ignorance of the cost of the latter. The flavor of the Partaga is too delicate for palates that have been accustomed to Connecticut seed leaf. So it is with humor. The finer it is in quality, the more danger of its not being recognized at all. Even Mark Twain has been taken in by an English review of his *Innocents Abroad*. Mark Twain is by no means a coarse humorist, but the Englishman's humor is so much finer than his, that he mistakes it for solid earnest, and 'larfs most consumedly.'

A man who cannot learn stands in his own light. Hereafter, when I write an article which I know to be good, but which I may have reason to fear will not, in some quarters, be considered to amount to much, coming from an American, I will aver that an Englishman wrote it and that it is copied from a London journal. And then I will occupy a back seat and enjoy the cordial applause.

(Still later)

(Twain's "review" will not die ... he's still laughing as he discovers yet another clip...)

"Mark Twain at last sees that the *Saturday Review*'s criticism of his *Innocents Abroad* was not serious, and he is intensely mortified at the thought of having been so badly sold. He takes the only course left him, and in the last *Galaxy* claims that he wrote the criticism himself, and published it in *The Galaxy* to sell the public. This is ingenious, but unfortunately it is not true. If any of our readers will take the trouble to call at this office we will show them the original article in the *Saturday Review* of October 8th, which, on comparison, will be found to be identical with the one published in *The Galaxy*. The best thing for Mark to do will be to admit that he was sold, and say no more about it."

The above is from the *Cincinnati Enquirer*, and is a falsehood. Come to the proof. If the Enquirer people, through any agent, will produce at *The Galaxy* office a *London Saturday Review* of October 8th, containing an "article which, on comparison, will be found to be that identical with the one published in *The Galaxy*, I will pay to that agent five hundred dollars cash. Moreover, if at any specified time I fail to produce at the same place a copy of the *London Saturday Review* of October 8th, containing a lengthy criticism upon the *Innocents Abroad*, entirely different, in every paragraph and sentence, from the one I published in *The Galaxy*, I will pay to the Enquirer agent another five hundred dollars cash. I offer Sheldon & Co., publishers, 500 Broadway, New York, as my "backers."

Any one in New York, authorized by the *Enquirer*, will receive prompt attention. It is an easy and profitable way for the *Enquirer* people to prove that they have not uttered a pitiful, deliberate falsehood in the above paragraphs. Will they swallow that falsehood ignominiously, or will they send an agent to *The Galaxy* office? I think the *Cincinnati Enquirer* must be edited by children.

Commentary

Keeping a delightfully stiff upper lip, Mark Twain opens as if he is some other writer, talking about himself in the third person, the better to make us think someone else is writing this: "Perhaps the most successful flights of humor of Mark Twain have been descriptions of the persons who did not appreciate his humor at all," the article begins. "...We have heard of the Pennsylvania clergyman who sadly returned his *Innocents Abroad* to the book-agent with the remark that 'the man who could shed tears over the tomb of Adam must be an idiot.'

Whether there really was a Pennsylvania clergyman or not, Twain manages a) to get in a joke about Adam's tomb (like the "Innocents" author was really crying over the mythical tomb; talk about not getting it) AND b) Twain sort of lets us in on the joke, winning us to his side against the dumb clergyman. Clever.

Appendix B

Again, he finds a way to charm his readers, explaining that he just HAS to share "the *Saturday Review's* article (on his book *Innocents Abroad* in full..." I dearly wanted to do it, for I cannot write anything half so delicious myself. If I had a cast-iron dog that could read this English criticism and preserve his austerity, I would drive him off the door-step.)" In other words, this joke is just too rich ... we have to share it. You can sense a writer on the verge of a great idea—one he can't wait to write down for us.

"Will the reader longer marvel at the brutal ignorance that pervades the American nation [Remember: He's writing as a British author.] when we tell him that we are informed upon perfectly good authority that this extravagant compilation of falsehoods, this exhaustless mine of stupendous lies, this *Innocents Abroad*, has actually been adopted by the schools and colleges of several of the states as a text-book! But if his falsehoods are distressing, his innocence and his ignorance are enough to make one burn the book and despise the author."

So ... the critic isn't just ripping Twain, he's ripping America. Well, what do you think about that?

The critic goes on, listing a series of Twain jokes from "Innocents" that he just doesn't get (knowing of course, we do). Reading these jokes now, it sounds like an early version of *The Daily Show*. Twain's influence is everywhere.

Perhaps my favorite example—and, I bet Twain's—is when he visits the ancient Roman city of Pompeii, the city buried in Vesuvius' famed eruption. The cobblestone streets aren't easy passage and ... well, let the critic tell us: "He hurts his foot in a rut two thousand years old in exhumed Pompeii, and presently, when staring at one of the cinder-like corpses unearthed in the next square, conceives the idea that maybe it is the remains of the ancient Street Commissioner, and straightway his horror softens down to a sort of chirpy contentment with the condition of things.... The book is absolutely dangerous, considering the magnitude and variety of its misstatements, and the convincing confidence with which they are made. And yet it is a text-book in the schools of America."

Innocents Abroad, of course, was not a textbook anywhere. But by Twain throwing that Anglophile dig, he wins even more readers to his side. Remember, he's writing this only a hundred years after the American Revolution.

Selected Short Works by Twain, with Annotations

Questions for Your Students

1. In your view, why did Mark Twain think it would be funny to critique his own book?
2. What did you notice about the writing style of the critic?
3. Why, in your view, did Twain include so many examples from *Innocents Abroad*?
4. Did the reactions of the *Cincinnati Inquirer* to this story confirm or go against Twain's depiction of literary critics? Explain.
5. If you were a newspaper reader at the time, looking at the Saturday Review article, what would you have thought?

"Fenimore Cooper's Literary Offenses": Twain Goes After One of America's Early Literary Stars

Author's note: By 1895, Mark Twain was an American institution. He was popular, wealthy, and his books were famous all over the world. But the one thing he didn't have was much support from the American literati. They acknowledged his success and his popular works like The Adventures of Tom Sawyer *and* Life on the Mississippi *and knew he had a vast worldwide audience. But if there were any critics or professors around who considered Twain as one of America's greatest living writers, well, they kept it to themselves. History does not record where or when or how Twain happened to come across some academic types writing in praise of a predecessor, James Fenimore Cooper. Twain's response to their work was simply legendary.*

Cooper was an early American writer, just a few years ahead of Twain, who was famous for his Leatherstocking Series, featuring the adventures of Natty Bumppo, a mythical American woodsman, Indian fighter and all-around hero. With novels like Last of the Mohicans *and* The Deerslayer, *Cooper mythologized the life of the pioneers in upstate New York, attempting to bring civilization to the American wilderness.*

Mark Twain took a somewhat more skeptical view of Cooper's work.

This article was written just about 10 years after Twain (real name: Samuel Clemens) had written Huckleberry Finn, *his not-quite-yet-acknowledged masterpiece. Nowadays,* Huckleberry Finn *is recognized not only as Twain's finest work; some call it the best American novel. At that time, Huck didn't have that sort of a literary reputation, which might have angered Twain.*

135

Appendix B

There were other factors. By 1895, Twain's financial troubles had already forced him to move out of his extravagant and wonderfully strange Hartford house. He was in debt, his literary reputation hadn't really gone anywhere in a while and he was winding down, career-wise.

You imagine one afternoon he was sitting around, probably smoking a cigar, when he read something that irked him. Grated on him. Got him hot. He had to say something. (No Twitter, remember!) An array of literary critics and college educators had written some lovely things about Cooper, a writer famous for his "Leatherstocking Tales" of adventures in the Indian wars in upstate, pre–Revolution New York. When one of these critics suggested, (probably after a big swallow) that "Cooper (was) the greatest artist in the domain of romantic fiction yet produced by America," why ... them was fightin' words to Mark Twain.

To exact his literary revenge in the essay we'll look at, Twain began by cleverly using their own words to hang them. He lays their quotes down like a string of bear traps to begin this literary roast. As you read 'em, you can imagine him chuckling to himself—and puffing big clouds of cigar smoke.

"Fenimore Cooper's Literary Offenses"

"*The Pathfinder* (1840) and *The Deerslayer* (1841) stand at the head of Cooper's novels as artistic creations. There are others of his works which contain parts as perfect as are to be found in these, and scenes even more thrilling. Not one can be compared with either of them as a finished whole.The defects in both of these tales are comparatively slight. They were pure works of art." —Prof. Lounsbury

"The five tales reveal an extraordinary fullness of invention.... One of the very greatest characters in fiction, Natty Bumppo.... The craft of the woodsman, the tricks of the trapper, all the delicate art of the forest, were familiar to Cooper from his youth up." —Prof. Brander Matthews

"Cooper is the greatest artist in the domain of romantic fiction yet produced by America." —Wilkie Collins

* * * * * * *

[*Twain intends these asterisks as smirks, don't you think? These bits of prose, taken out of context seem positively purplish, which was Twain's intent. He knows we can't wait to hear what he thinks about them.*]

Selected Short Works by Twain, with Annotations

It seems to me that it was far from right for the Professor of English Literature in Yale, the Professor of English Literature in Columbia, and Wilkie Collins to deliver opinions on Cooper's literature *without having read some of it*. [*Bang!*] It would have been much more decorous to keep silent and let persons talk who have read Cooper. Cooper's art has some defects.[*Understatement alert*] In one place in *Deerslayer*, and in the restricted space of two-thirds of a page, Cooper has scored 114 offences against literary art out of a possible 115. It breaks the record.

[*Is he exaggerating about the 114 of 115? Probably. Does it set up what Twain intends next—hinting that he's going to show us some of these gaffes? So the reader has a road map for where the writer is going right away! Very good idea for us, too! Show the reader where you are going.*]

There are nineteen rules governing literary art in the domain of romantic fiction—some say twenty-two. In *Deerslayer* Cooper violated eighteen of them. These require:

1. That a tale shall accomplish something and arrive somewhere. But the *Deerslayer* tale accomplishes nothing and arrives in the air. 2. They require that the episodes of a tale shall be necessary parts of the tale, and shall help to develop it. But as the *Deerslayer* tale is not a tale, and accomplishes nothing and arrives nowhere, the episodes have no rightful place in the work, since there was nothing for them to develop. 3. They require that the personages in a tale shall be alive, except in the case of corpses, and that always the reader shall be able to tell the corpses from the others. But this detail has often been overlooked in the *Deerslayer* tale.

[*Notice the tone—the feeling you get from Twain's word choices, his literary voice? Notice the parallel structure adds to the comic effect as each sentence is constructed the same way. Is he outraged that these critics are throwing these bouquets to someone else? Is he laughing as he writes?— Cooper isn't!*]

4. They require that the personages in a tale, both dead and alive, shall exhibit a sufficient excuse for being there. But this detail also has been overlooked in the *Deerslayer* tale.

5. They require that when the personages of a tale deal in conversation, the talk shall sound like human talk, and be talk such as human beings would be likely to talk in the given circumstances, and have a discoverable meaning, also a discoverable purpose, and a show of relevancy, and remain in the neighborhood of the subject in hand, and be

Appendix B

interesting to the reader, and help out the tale, and stop when the people cannot think of anything more to say. But this requirement has been ignored from the beginning of the *Deerslayer* tale to the end of it.

6. They require that when the author describes the character of a personage in his tale, the conduct and conversation of that personage shall justify said description. But this law gets little or no attention in the *Deerslayer* tale, as Natty Bumppo's case will amply prove. They require that when a personage talks like an illustrated, gilt-edged, tree-calf, hand-tooled, seven-dollar Friendship's Offering in the beginning of a paragraph, he shall not talk like a negro minstrel in the end of it. But this rule is flung down and danced upon in the *Deerslayer* tale.

[*Can't you hear Jon Stewart's voice? Or David Letterman? Think Twain was an influence? Yes? Go to the head of the class! Isn't this fun? Now this is literary analysis, believe it or not! We are breaking down another writer's work, asking questions and having a few laughs. Twain not only knows how to write, he also knows how to make us laugh. He shows both here, giving impeccable advice.*]

8. They require that crass stupidities shall not be played upon the reader as "the craft of the woodsman, the delicate art of the forest," by either the author or the people in the tale. But this rule is persistently violated in the *Deerslayer* tale.

9. They require that the personages of a tale shall confine themselves to possibilities and let miracles alone; or, if they venture a miracle, the author must so plausibly set it forth as to make it look possible and reasonable. But these rules are not respected in the *Deerslayer* tale.

10. They require that the author shall make the reader feel a deep interest in the personages of his tale and in their fate; and that he shall make the reader love the good people in the tale and hate the bad ones. But the reader of the *Deerslayer* tale dislikes the good people in it, is indifferent to the others, and wishes they would all get drowned together.

[*Notice the writer's voice is consistent. He admits he "wishes they would all get drowned together." He's on a roll. We know he's going to do, don't we? Right again! He's going to show us how Cooper violates these rules, right? He sets up our expectations—then delivers. That satisfies a reader. We have the rules, how about the violations? An expert writer, Twain is happy to nit-pick.*]

Cooper's gift in the way of invention was not a rich endowment; but such as it was he liked to work it, he was pleased with the effects, and indeed he did some quite sweet things with it. In his little box of stage properties he kept six or eight cunning devices, tricks, artifices for his savages and woodsmen to deceive and circumvent each other with, and he was never so happy as when he was working these innocent things and seeing them go.

A favorite one was to make a moccasined person tread in the tracks of the moccasined enemy, and thus hide his own trail. Cooper wore out barrels and barrels of moccasins in working that trick. Another stage-property that he pulled out of his box pretty frequently was his broken twig. He prized his broken twig above all the rest of his effects, and worked it the hardest. It is a restful chapter in any book of his when somebody doesn't step on a dry twig and alarm all the reds and whites for two hundred yards around. Every time a Cooper person is in peril, and absolute silence is worth four dollars a minute, he is sure to step on a dry twig. There may be a hundred handier things to step on, but that wouldn't satisfy Cooper. Cooper requires him to turn out and find a dry twig; and if he can't do it, go and borrow one. In fact, the Leather Stocking Series ought to have been called the Broken Twig Series.

[*Notice the writer's voice is again, consistent and critical. As Twain says, "when absolute silence is worth four dollars a minute, (Cooper) is sure to step on a dry twig...." When you are examining argumentative writing for logos (logic), ethos (character) or pathos (emotion) here is one of the logos entries. And Twain goes a little further with that in just a bit.*]

I am sorry that there is not room to put in a few dozen instances of the delicate art of the forest, as practiced by Natty Bumppo and some of the other Cooperian experts. Perhaps we may venture two or three samples. Cooper was a sailor—a naval officer; yet he gravely tells us how a vessel, driving toward a lee shore in a gale, is steered for a particular spot by her skipper because he knows of an *undertow* there which will hold her back against the gale and save her. For just pure woodcraft, or sailor-craft, or whatever it is, isn't that neat? For several years, Cooper was daily in the society of artillery, and he ought to have noticed that when a cannon-ball strikes the ground it either buries itself or skips a hundred feet or so; skips again a hundred feet or so—and so on, till finally it gets tired and rolls. Now in one place he loses some "females"—as he always calls women—in the edge of a wood near a plain at night in a fog, on purpose to give Bumppo a chance to show off the delicate art of the forest before the reader. These mislaid people are hunting for a fort. They hear a cannon-blast, and a cannon-ball presently comes rolling into the wood

Appendix B

and stops at their feet. To the females this suggests nothing. The case is very different with the admirable Bumppo. I wish I may never know peace again if he doesn't strike out promptly and *follow the track* of that cannonball across the plain in the dense fog and find the fort. Isn't it a daisy?

If Cooper had any real knowledge of Nature's ways of doing things, he had a most delicate art in concealing the fact. For instance: one of his acute Indian experts, Chingachgook (pronounced Chicago, I think), has lost the trail of a person he is tracking through the forest. Apparently that trail is hopelessly lost. Neither you nor I could ever have guessed the way to find it. It was very different with Chicago. Chicago was not stumped for long. He turned a running stream out of its course, and there, in the slush in its old bed, were that person's moccasin tracks. The current did not wash them away, as it would have done in all other like cases—no, even the eternal laws of Nature have to vacate when Cooper wants to put up a delicate job of woodcraft on the reader.

We must be a little wary when Brander Matthews tells us that Cooper's books "reveal an extraordinary fullness of invention." As a rule, I am quite willing to accept Brander Matthews's literary judgments and applaud his lucid and graceful phrasing of them; but that particular statement needs to be taken with a few tons of salt.

[*Is this little note to Brander Matthews the REASON Twain was inspired to write this article? It's a good question and despite the massive Mark Twain Autobiography series—three volumes that would give you a hernia—one that is unanswered.*]

Bless your heart, Cooper hadn't any more invention than a horse; and don't mean a high-class horse, either; I mean a clothes-horse. It would be very difficult to find a clever "situation" in Cooper's books, and still more difficult to find one of any kind which has failed to render absurd by his handling of it. Look at the episodes of "the caves"; and at the celebrated scuffle between Maqua and those others on the table-land a few days later; and at Hurry Harry's queer water-transit from the castle to the ark; and at Deerslayer's half-hour with his first corpse; and at the quarrel between Hurry Harry and Deerslayer later; and at—but choose for yourself; you can't go amiss.

[*This next section was excerpted on the AP language and composition test a while ago and is an excellent example of a writer using* logos, *or, logic, to show how Cooper's conceptions for these event is just not logical or possible.*]

If Cooper had been an observer his inventive faculty would have worked better; not more interestingly, but more rationally, more plausibly. Cooper's proudest creations in the way of "situations" suffer noticeably from the absence of the observer's protecting gift. Cooper's eye was splendidly inaccurate. Cooper seldom saw anything correctly. He saw nearly all things as through a glass eye, darkly. Of course a man who cannot see the commonest little every-day matters accurately is working at a disadvantage when he is constructing a "situation." In the *Deerslayer* tale Cooper has a stream which is fifty feet wide where it flows out of a lake; it presently narrows to twenty as it meanders along for no given reason, and yet when a stream acts like that it ought to be required to explain itself. Fourteen pages later the width of the brook's outlet from the lake has suddenly shrunk thirty feet, and become "the narrowest part of the stream." This shrinkage is not accounted for. The stream has bends in it, a sure indication that it has alluvial banks and cuts them; yet these bends are only thirty and fifty feet long. If Cooper had been a nice and punctilious observer he would have noticed that the bends were often nine hundred feet long than short of it.

Cooper made the exit of that stream fifty feet wide, in the first place, for no particular reason; in the second place, he narrowed it to less than twenty to accommodate some Indians. He bends a "sapling" to form an arch over this narrow passage, and conceals six Indians in its foliage. They are "laying" for a settler's scow or ark which is coming up the stream on its way to the lake; it is being hauled against the stiff current by rope whose stationary end is anchored in the lake; its rate of progress cannot be more than a mile an hour. Cooper describes the ark, but pretty obscurely. In the matter of dimensions "it was little more than a modern canal boat." Let us guess, then, that it was about one hundred and forty feet long. It was of "greater breadth than common." Let us guess then that it was about sixteen feet wide. This leviathan had been prowling down bends which were but a third as long as itself, and scraping between banks where it only had two feet of space to spare on each side. We cannot too much admire this miracle. A low- roofed dwelling occupies "two-thirds of the ark's length"— a dwelling ninety feet long and sixteen feet wide, let us say—a kind of vestibule train. The dwelling has two rooms—each forty- five feet long and sixteen feet wide, let us guess. One of them is the bedroom of the Hutter girls, Judith and Hetty; the other is the parlor in the daytime, at night it is papa's bedchamber. The ark is arriving at the stream's exit now, whose width has been reduced to less than twenty feet to accommodate

Appendix B

the Indians—say to eighteen. There is a foot to spare on each side of the boat. Did the Indians notice that there was going to be a tight squeeze there? Did they notice that they could make money by climbing down out of that arched sapling and just stepping aboard when the ark scraped by? No, other Indians would have noticed these things, but Cooper's Indian's never notice anything. Cooper thinks they are marvelous creatures for noticing, but he was almost always in error about his Indians. There was seldom a sane one among them. The ark is one hundred and forty-feet long; the dwelling is ninety feet long. The idea of the Indians is to drop softly and secretly from the arched sapling to the dwelling as the ark creeps along under it at the rate of a mile an hour, and butcher the family. It will take the ark a minute and a half to pass under. It will take the ninety-foot dwelling a minute to pass under. Now, then, what did the six Indians do? It would take you thirty years to guess, and even then you would have to give it up, I believe. Therefore, I will tell you what the Indians did. Their chief, a person of quite extraordinary intellect for a Cooper Indian, warily watched the canal-boat as it squeezed along under him and when he had got his calculations fined down to exactly the right shade, as he judge, he let go and dropped. And *missed the boat*! That is actually what he did. He missed the house, and landed in he stern of the scow. It was not much of a fall, yet it knocked him silly. He lay there unconscious. If the house had been ninety-seven feet long he would have made the trip. The error lay in the construction of the house. Cooper was no architect. There still remained in the roost five Indians. The boat has passed under and is now out of their reach. Let me explain what the five did—you would not be able to reason it out for yourself. No. 1 jumped for the boat, but fell in the water astern of it. Then No. 2 jumped for the boat, but fell in the water still further astern of it. Then No. 3 jumped for the boat, and fell a good way astern of it. Then No. 4 jumped for the boat, and fell in the water *away* astern. Then even No. 5 made a jump for the boat—for he was Cooper Indian. In that matter of intellect, the difference between a Cooper Indian and the Indian that stands in front of the cigar-shop is not spacious.

[*"The difference between a Cooper Indian and the Indian that stands in front of the cigar-shop is not spacious"* Hahaha! Who else would have thought to use the word "spacious" right there? *"The difference between the right word and the almost right word is the difference between lightning and the lightning bug."*]

The scow episode is really a sublime burst of invention; but it does not thrill, because the inaccuracy of details throw a sort of air of fictitiousness and general improbability over it. This comes of Cooper's inadequacy as observer.

[*It's clear by now, Twain has made his point—and then some. But he can't stop himself. Cooper's critical reputation never really recovered from this Twain blast. There are still people, Cooper fans (and perhaps relatives) who try and defend him. Twain's case, however, is convincing. He's fortunate that no one in his lifetime ever took apart the ending of* Huckleberry Finn *in similar fashion.*]

The reader will find some examples of Cooper's high talent for inaccurate observation in the account of the shooting-match in *The Pathfinder*.

A common wrought nail was driven lightly into the target, its head having been first touched with paint.

The color of the paint is not stated—an important omission, but Cooper deals freely in important omissions. No, after all, it was not an important omission; for this nail-head is *a hundred yards from* the marksmen, and could not be seen at that distance, no matter what its color might be. How far can the best eyes see a common housefly? A hundred yards? It is quite impossible. Very well; eyes that cannot see a house-fly that is a hundred yards away cannot see an ordinary nail-head at that distance, for the size of the two objects is the same. It takes a keen eye to see a fly or a nail-head at fifty yards—one hundred and fifty-feet. Can the reader do it?

The nail was lightly driven, its head painted, and game called. Then the Cooper miracles began. The bullet of the first marksman chipped an edge of the nail-head; the next man's bullet drove the nail a little way into the target—and removed all the paint. Haven't the miracles gone far enough now? Not to suit Cooper; for the purpose of this whole scheme is to show off his prodigy, Deerslayer-Hawkeye-Long-Rifle-Leatherstocking-Pathfinder-Bumppo before the ladies.

"*Be all ready to clench it, boys!*" *cried out Pathfinder, stepping into his friend's tracks the instant they were vacant.* "*Never mind a new nail; I can see that, though the paint is gone, and what I can see I can hit at a hundred yards, though it were only a mosquito's eye. Be ready to clench!*"

The rifle cracked, the bullet sped its way, and the head of the nail was buried in the wood, covered by the piece of flattened lead.

There, you see, is a man who could hunt flies with a rifle, and command a ducal salary in a Wild West show to-day if we had him back with us.

The recorded feat is certainly surprising just as it stands; but it is not

Appendix B

surprising enough for Cooper. Cooper adds a touch. He has made Pathfinder do this miracle with another man's rife; and not only that, but Pathfinder did not have even the advantage of loading it himself. He had everything against him, and yet he made that impossible shot; and not only made it, but did it with absolute confidence, saying, "Be ready to clench." Now a person like that would have undertaken that same feat with a brickbat, and with Cooper to help he would have achieved it, too.

Pathfinder showed off handsomely that day before the ladies. His very first feat a thing which no Wild West show can touch. He was standing with the group of marksmen, observing—a hundred yards from the target, mind; one Jasper Rasper raised his rifle and drove the center of the bull's-eye. Then the Quartermaster fired. The target exhibited no result this time. There was a laugh. "It's a dead miss," said Major Lundie. Pathfinder waited an impressive moment or two; then said, in that calm, indifferent, know-it-all way of his, "No, Major, he has covered Jasper's bullet, as will be seen if any one will take the trouble to examine the target."

Wasn't it remarkable! How *could* he see that little pellet fly through the air and enter that distant bullet-hole? Yet that is what he did; for nothing is impossible to a Cooper person. Did any of those people have any deep-seated doubts about this thing? No; for that would imply sanity, and these were all Cooper people.

The respect for Pathfinder's skill and for his quickness and accuracy of sight [the italics are mine] was so profound and general, that the instant he made this declaration the spectators began to distrust their own opinions, and a dozen rushed to the target in order to ascertain the fact. There, sure enough, it was found that the Quartermaster's bullet had gone through the hole made by Jasper's, and that, too, so accurately as to require a minute examination to be certain of the circumstance, which, however, was soon clearly established by discovering one bullet over the other in the stump against which the target was placed.

They made a "minute" examination; but never mind, how could they know that there were two bullets in that hole without digging the latest one out? for neither probe nor eyesight could prove the presence of any more than one bullet. Did they dig? No; as we shall see. It is the Pathfinder's turn now; he steps out before the ladies, takes aim, and fires.

But, alas! here is a disappointment; in incredible, an unimaginable disappointment—for the target's aspect is unchanged; there is nothing there but that same old bullet hole!

Selected Short Works by Twain, with Annotations

"If one dared to hint at such a thing," cried Major Duncan, "I should say that the Pathfinder has also missed the target."

As nobody had missed it yet, the "also" was not necessary; but never mind about that, for the Pathfinder is going to speak.

"No, no, Major," said he, confidently, "that would be a risky declaration. I didn't load the piece, and can't say what was in it; but if it was lead, you will find the bullet driving down those of the Quartermaster and Jasper, else is not my name Pathfinder."

A shout from the target announced the truth of this assertion.

Is the miracle sufficient as it stands? Not for Cooper. The Pathfinder speaks again, as he "now slowly advances toward the stage occupied by the females":

"That's not all, boys, that's not all; if you find the target touched at all, I'll own to a miss. The Quartermaster cut the wood, but you'll find no wood cut by that last messenger."

The miracle is at last complete. He knew—doubtless *saw* — at the distance of a hundred yards—this his bullet had passed into the hole *without fraying the edges*. There were now three bullets in that one hole—three bullets embedded processionally in the body of the stump back of the target. Everybody knew this—somehow or other—and yet nobody had dug any of them out to make sure. Cooper is not a close observer, but he is interesting. He is certainly always that, no matter what happens. And he is more interesting when he is not noticing what he is about than when he is. This is a considerable merit.

[*And still more. Cooper's lame conversations...*]

The conversations in the Cooper books have a curious sound in our modern ears. To believe that such talk really ever came out of people's mouths would be to believe that there was a time when time was of no value to a person who thought he had something to say; when it was the custom to spread a two-minute remark out to ten; when a man's mouth was a rolling-mill, and busied itself all day long in turning four-foot pigs of thought into thirty-foot bars of conversational railroad iron by attenuation; when subjects were seldom faithfully stuck to, but the talk wandered all around and arrived nowhere; when conversations consisted mainly of irrelevancies, with here and there a relevancy, a relevancy with an embarrassed look, as not being able to explain how it got there.

Cooper was certainly not a master in the construction of dialogue. Inaccurate observation defeated him here as it defeated him in so many

Appendix B

other enterprises of his life. He even failed to notice that the man who talks corrupt English six days in the week must and will talk it on seventh, and can't help himself. In the *Deerslayer* story, he lets Deerslayer talk the showiest kind of book-talk sometimes, and at other times the basest of base dialects. For instance, when some one asks him if he has a sweetheart, and if so, where she abides, this is his majestic answer:

"She's in the forest—hanging from the boughs of the trees, in a soft rain—in the dew on the open grass—the clouds that float about in the blue heavens—the birds that sing in the woods—the sweet springs where I slake my thirst—and in all the other glorious gifts that come from God's Providence!"

And he preceded that, a little before, with this:

"It consarns me as all things that touches a friend consarns a friend."

And this is another of his remarks:

"If I was Injin born, now, I might tell of this, or carry in the scalp and boast of the expl'ite afore the whole tribe; of if my inimy had only been a bear"—[and so on]

We cannot imagine such a thing as a veteran Scotch Commander-in-Chief comporting himself like a windy melodramatic actor, but Cooper could. On one occasion, Alice and Cora were being chased by the French through a fog in the neighborhood of their father's fort:

"Point de quartier aux coquins! cried an eager pursuer, who seemed to direct the operations of the enemy.

"Stand firm and be ready, my gallant 60ths!" suddenly exclaimed a voice above them; "wait to see the enemy, fire low, and sweep the glacis."

"Father! father" exclaimed a piercing cry from out the mist. "It is I! Alice! thy own Elsie! spare, O! save your daughters!"

"Hold!" shouted the former speaker, in the awful tones of parental agony, the sound reaching even to the woods, and rolling back in a solemn echo. "'Tis she! God has restored me my children! Throw open the sally-port; to the field, 60ths, to the field! pull not a trigger, lest ye kill my lambs! Drive off these dogs of France with your steel!"

Cooper's word-sense was singularly dull. When a person has a poor ear for music he will flat and sharp right along without knowing it. He keeps near the tune, but is *not* the tune. When a person has a poor ear for words, the result is a literary flatting and sharping; you perceive what he is intending to say, but you also perceive that he does not *say* it. This is Cooper. He was not a word-musician. His ear was satisfied with the *approximate* words. I will furnish some circumstantial evidence in support of this charge. My instances are gathered from half a dozen pages of the tale called *Deerslayer*. He uses "Verbal" for "oral"; "precision" for "facility"; "phenomena" for "marvels"; "necessary" for "predetermined"; "unsophisticated" for "primitive"; "preparation" for "expectancy"; "rebuked" for "subdued"; "dependent on" for "resulting from"; "fact" for "condition"; "fact" for "conjecture"; "precaution" for "caution"; "explain" for "determine"; "mortified" for "disappointed"; "meretricious" for "factitious"; "materially" for "considerably"; "decreasing" for "deepening"; "increasing" for "disappearing"; "embedded" for "inclosed"; "treacherous" for "hostile"; "stood" for "stooped"; "softened" for "replaced"; "rejoined" for "remarked"; "situation" for "condition"; "different" for "differing"; "insensible" for "unsentient"; "brevity" for "celerity"; "distrusted" for "suspicious"; "mental imbecility" for "imbecility"; "eyes" for "sight"; "counteracting" for "opposing"; "funeral obsequies" for "obsequies."

There have been daring people in the world who claimed that Cooper could write English, but they are all dead now—all dead but Lounsbury. I don't remember that Lounsbury makes the claim in so many words, still he makes it, for he says that *Deerslayer* is a "pure work of art." Pure, in that connection, means faultless—faultless in all details—and language is a detail. If Mr. Lounsbury had only compared Cooper's English with the English he writes himself—but it is plain that he didn't; and so it is likely that he imagines until this day that Cooper's is as clean and compact as his own. Now I feel sure, deep down in my heart, that Cooper wrote about the poorest English that exists in our language, and that the English of *Deerslayer* is the very worst that even Cooper ever wrote.

I may be mistaken, but it does seem to me that *Deerslayer* is not a work of art in any sense; it does seem to me that it is destitute of every detail that goes to the making of a work of art; in truth, it seems to me that *Deerslayer* is just simply a literary *delirium tremens*.

A work of art? It has no invention; it has no order, system, sequence, or result; it has no lifelikeness, no thrill, no stir, no seeming of reality; its characters are confusedly drawn, and by their acts and words they prove that they are not the sort of people the author claims that they are; its humor is pathetic; its pathos is funny; its conversations are—oh! indescribable; its love-scenes odious; its English a crime against the language.

Counting these out, what is left is Art. I think we must all admit that.

Appendix B

The Teaching Points: What Can You Do with Your Students?

Twain ends, of course, on a laugh. Do you think Twain had as much fun writing it as we did reading and analyzing it? True, Cooper's professional reputation was never quite the same again. Was Twain fair? Did he need to be? What IS the critic's role? Hmmm. Topic for another day?

Assignment: try to write your own version of Twain's essay. Start with the excerpts we used as a springboard. What are we looking for?:

- Find something to say.
- Say it in a clear, consistent voice—a tone that is YOU.
- Have fun with it. Writing—sharing your ideas with someone—should be fun. (You like texting, don't you?)
- Stretch these ideas out. See where your brain takes you.
- (Oh, yes ... and smile. Worked for Twain, didn't it?

Final hint: what if *we* "modeled" one way you could begin your essay? Would that help you get started? You got it!

Here goes... (Your teacher takes the pen...)

Imagine, if you will, the collected literary work of American novelist James Fenimore Cooper as some sort of strange castle; ill-conceived, oddly constructed with bad landscaping, rotten plumbing and an overpowering odor. In his relentless essay, "Fenimore Cooper's Literary Offenses," Mark Twain not only sacks Cooper's castle, but critiques its architecture, drains its moat, breaks all the windows, throws a cherry bomb into center court and suggests that even its ghosts have lisps. A more vigorous, comprehensive dismissal of a literary figure is difficult to imagine.

Twain doesn't miss a thing, blasting Cooper's implausible characters, their halting, unbelievable dialogues, his creaky, and barely credible plot lines. Twain dissects Cooper's prose under such an unrelenting microscope, questioning all the way down to his very word choice, if there had been a way to criticize the size of the periods in Cooper's punctuation, you get the sense Twain would have had at that, too.

Cooper's work is not all that comes within range of Twain's invective. He begins his essay with four quotes from literary experts of the time, pinning them under their verbal bouquets like a Monarch butterfly struggling under a pair of straight house pins. "Cooper is the greatest artist in the domain of romantic fiction yet produced by America," Twain says,

Selected Short Works by Twain, with Annotations

quoting Wilkie Collins. "The craft of the woodsman, the tricks of the trapper, all the delicate art of the forest.." claims Professor Brander Matthews—words that Twain will use against Matthews, Cooper and the entire literary establishment and their misguided (and to Twain) wholly inexplicable praise for this literary disaster case. As Twain suggests in his down-to-earth opening sentence: "It seems to me far from right for Professor(s)… to deliver opinions on Cooper's literature without having read some of it." And the laughs begin.

Appendix C: Additional Twain-Related Assignments

If you're a Mark Twain fan—and how could read this far and not be?—you may remember this delightful little addendum regarding the weather in his books. Apply that here…

> "Of course, weather is necessary to a narrative of human experience. That is conceded. But it ought to be put where it will not be in the way; where it will not interrupt the flow of the narrative. And it ought to be the ablest weather that can be had, not ignorant, poor-quality, amateur weather. Weather is a literary specialty, and no untrained hand can turn out a good article of it. The present author can do only a few trifling ordinary kinds of weather, and he cannot do those very good. So it has seemed wisest to borrow such weather as is necessary for the book from qualified and recognized experts—giving credit, of course. This weather will be found over in the back part of the book, out of the way. See Appendix. The reader is requested to turn over and help himself from time to time as he goes along." —Mark Twain

Assignment One: Bloom's Taxonomy

REMEMBER: Quizzes to test students' memory/recall of pertinent information from *Huckleberry Finn*.

UNDERSTAND: Discuss Twain's use of the "N" word in the early chapters.

APPLY: Explain Twain's author's purpose for his ugly depiction of Pap.

ANALYZE: Compare/Contrast Huck's actions in Chapters 14–15.

EVALUATE: Was Huck right to not turn Jim in?

CREATE: Imagine a Huck-Jim discussion on some other topic NOT covered in *Huckleberry Finn*.

Additional Twain-Related Assignments

Assignment Two: Huck Finn Chapters 8–9 Quiz

(Write in your journal)

1. What device does Mark Twain brilliantly use to once again raise the issue of religion/prayer early in chapter eight?
2. How does Huck first discover someone else is on Jackson's Island?
3. Why does Jim decide to run away?
4. How does Jim react to first seeing Huck?
5. Why, after he's established that Huck is not dead, is Jim still suspicious of witchcraft from Huck?
6. What had Jim had to eat since being on Jackson's Island?
7. Why didn't Jim steal a skiff (small boat) as he explained it?
8. Why is Jim "rich"?
9. What are two of Jim's "signs"?
10. What happens in chapter nine?

Assignment Three: Two Sides of Twain

Today, we're going to look at two successive chapters in *Huckleberry Finn* that capture the genius of Mark Twain in a way that perhaps no two other successive chapters in the book do.

In chapter fourteen, Huck and Jim, now getting well acquainted with one another, delve into a discussion of all sorts of things, which is comical—but with a point about each character.

In chapter fifteen, after the rollicking fun of the previous chapter, Twain puts Huck through the first of several heart-wrenching moral crises. Brilliantly, he puts us in Huck's shoes, makes us wonder what we would do in a similar circumstance.

Questions for Writers

- In chapter fourteen, Mark Twain walks a fine line, making fun of someone's lack of education without, I believe, making fun of the uneducated person. Explain how, as a writer, Twain achieves that.
- In chapter fifteen, Huck sees an opportunity to take advantage of

Appendix C

Jim and does, then regrets it. Why, in your view, is this critical to understanding the relationship between Huck and Jim?
- Jim is not afraid to call Huck on his behavior. Explain how Jim's response and reaction would likely be different if Huck were a man.

Assignment Four: Research Assignment

The "N" Word and Huck Finn: A Controversy

Mark Twain's controversial novel, *The Adventures of Huckleberry Finn*, continues to stir the pot at American schools because of Twain's use of the "N" word. Having read the novel yourself, watch the four sources, use all of them in your three-page paper (a must) and write your response.

1. WATCH: Ronald Reagan Speech.
    a. URL: https://www.youtube.com/watch?v=V9f2_61GXR0.
2. WATCH: *60 Minutes* segment on new edition missing "N" word.
    a. URL: https://www.youtube.com/watch?v=nW9-qee1m9o.
3. WATCH: William Bennett on *Huck Finn*.
    a. URL: https://www.youtube.com/watch?v=Gm72cvq-f_E.
4. READ: How Mark Twain presented *Huck Finn* on the stage.
    a. URL: http://www.salon.com/2016/04/23/the_night_mark_twain_brought_huck_finn_alive/.

Assignment Five: Research Assignment: A Three-Page Paper

Huck's Lousy Ending: What Happened?

Though Twain's masterpiece has drawn the praise of critics the world over, the ending to the novel, where Jim, a free man, is subject to the whims of Tom Sawyer, has puzzled readers everywhere. Was Twain wrong, or was his ending misunderstood? Listen to Hogge's class, write a response to it and your own understanding/appreciation for the ending of the book in a 3-page paper.

1. WATCH: Bob Hogge's presentation at Weber State University on Huck's strange ending.

Additional Twain-Related Assignments

    a. URL: https://www.youtube.com/watch?v=-scFfGDBMnk.
2. READ: Jayne Ann Phillips' Afterword in our edition of *Huck Finn*.

Assignment Six: Project-Based Learning

Project-Idea List

CHOICES

    1. Create a full-sized front page of a newspaper that will highlight some of the memorable moments from the novel with headlines and short stories; Huck's tearing up the letter, the Grangerford feud, Huck's prank after the fog, Jim's escape, Tom's wound, etc.
    2. Create a music video about *Huckleberry Finn* and the lessons of the novel.
    3. Postcards from Huck. Imagine Huck sent postcards from the several stops he made as he and Jim went down the Mississippi. Make them funny, colorful, and informative.
    4. Create an original full-color book cover, including a jacket synopsis and author biography with a full, typed book review alongside.

Assignment Seven: Write Your Own Ending

(Double Points) Write Your Own Ending

    Writer David Bradley notes that many have criticized the ending of *Huck Finn*, but "none of them has been able to suggest—much less write—a better ending.... They failed for the same reason that Twain wrote the ending as he did: America has never been able to write a better ending. America has never been able to write any ending at all." What do you think he means? Ask students to imagine they were Mark Twain's editor and to write Twain a letter explaining why and how he should change the ending. (To extend this activity, have students actually rewrite the ending, and compare their versions to the original.) I would say you'd need to go as far as Huck reaching the Phelps' plantation. Try and keep the original spirit of the book in your mind.... Good luck.

Suggested Reading and Viewing

Burns, Ken, dir. *Mark Twain.* Walpole, NH: Florentine Films, 2002. DVD, 220 mins.

One of our great documentary filmmakers, it was a matter of time until Ken Burns got around to doing a documentary on the life of one of our greatest Americans, Mark Twain. When he did in a two-parter that debuted on PBS, it was worth the wait. The intriguing decision that Burns made was to use the crusty voice of actor Kevin Conway as Twain, instead of what might have been a more obvious choice, actor Hal Holbrook, who has been doing a one-man show, *Mark Twain Tonight,* for 50 years. This was an interesting decision because, as Burns explained, using Conway's voice as Twain freed up Holbrook to speak as a Twain expert, not just an impersonator. The documentary faithfully takes us through Twain's extraordinarily life with plenty of examples of his writing, narrated brilliantly by Conway. As you listen to the excerpts from Twain's first book, *Innocents Abroad,* his commentary is just so darn fresh and funny, you try and imagine what it read like in the real world at that time. It must have seemed like it was Mars.

For teaching purposes, Burns includes what many Twain scholars point to as an important and often overlooked turning point in the development of *Huckleberry Finn*. Burns offers a segment on Twain's "A True Story, Just As I Heard It," the heartbreaking saga, told in vernacular, of the life of the Clemens' servant, "Aunt Rachel." Some scholars think that this moving piece revealed to Twain the power inherent in vernacular speech as "Aunt Rachel" told of her most improbable mother and child reunion. As the DVD goes through Twain's work, Burns reaches out to writers and scholars like Arthur Miller, Hal Holbrook, Shelly Fishkin and many others to talk about the lasting impact of Twain's writing. The bits on *Huckleberry*

Suggested Reading and Viewing

Finn and *The Adventures of Tom Sawyer* are very good and suitable introductions to the work before you begin to read.

To me, the special features, and particularly the interview outtakes, were extraordinarily useful, particularly as you begin *Huck* and need to discuss the use of the "N" word. When they get to *Huckleberry Finn*, Holbrook, Fishkin and others directly address the use of the "N" word as being essential to Twain's purpose in writing the book. For my classes, hearing various Twain scholars talk about the use of the "N" word helps, I think, to soften the blow and give your classes a genuine sense of Twain's intent and moral vision. If you're planning on teaching *Huckleberry Finn*, I'd say this DVD is a must.

Geismar, Maxwell. *Mark Twain: An American Prophet.* Boston: Houghton Mifflin, 1970.

Geismar, a fly-in-the-ointment sort of writer, seemed to write this book to try and correct the image of Twain as he saw him. Or maybe a better way to say it is, he wrote it to intentionally contradict the standard Twain story as told by his early biographers and critics, people like Van Wyck Brooks, Bernard DeVoto, and Justin Kaplan, all those early writers who jumped on the Twain train. He loves the later Twain, the politically charged writer who criticized Teddy Roosevelt, American Imperialism and all sorts of things that seemed to run contrary to the funny man who wrote kids' books. Geismar sees Twain as a true, somewhat undiscovered—as hard as that is to believe—American artist, someone whose well worth reading and thinking and writing about. I think I'd read it shortly before Sr. Marjorie challenged me on *A Connecticut Yankee in King Arthur's Court*. It shaped the way I understood Twain and his impact on American letters. It may do the same for you.

Hal Holbrook: Mark Twain Tonight! New York: Vining/CBS-TV, 1967. DVD, 88 mins.

If you've never seen Hal Holbrook inhabit the character of Mark Twain as he does in this revelatory 90-minute program that first aired on CBS in 1967, skip *Game of Thrones* for a night and watch some real entertainment. Portraying Twain at about age 70, dressed in a natty white suit, smoking cigars on stage (something the real Twain would never do). Holbrook gets you acquainted with the literary giant that wisecracked his way from the wheel of a Mississippi riverboat into literary immortality with a delightfully cranky, funny, insightful lecture that you can sit and watch from start to finish, or use as a bell-ringer or writing challenge in class.

Having had the opportunity to see Holbrook's presentation in person four separate times over the years, the only criticism I'd have of this program is that it's not longer or that Holbrook has never done an updated video version of different Twain material. He has, reportedly, memorized hours and hours of Twain and has adapted the presentation to suit the current political climate. Twain's writing seems so on target, his comments are never dated and he's able to make you laugh—and think—at the same time. In this program, Twain talks about politics and religion, reads from *Huckleberry Finn*, and gives you a sense that you have shared 90 minutes with someone worth listening to. Filmmaker Scott Teems recently did a documentary *Holbrook/Twain: An American Odyssey* that drew all sorts of acclaim, but it has yet to be officially released to the buying public. That would be interesting to watch, as would be Holbrook's command performance at the White House in 2001, where he did *Mark Twain Tonight*. You assume somebody filmed it. Wouldn't it be great to see it?

Lettis, Richard, Robert F. McDonnell, and William E. Morris, eds. *Huck Finn and His Critics*. New York: Macmillan, 1962.

With a book like *Huck Finn*, you never know what you're going to find out there. I found this collection of critical essays on Twain's classic at a second-hand bookstore for $7. It was printed by Macmillan in 1962 and includes the novel followed by a series of critical articles from an all-star cast: Albert Bigelow Paine, Van Wyck Brooks, Bernard DeVoto, V.S. Pritchett, James T. Farrell, Lionel Trilling, Leo Marx, Richard P. Adams and several others. Since I'd read so many of the more recent reviews and appreciations of the novel, it was interesting to look back 50 years or so and see what the critical climate was like then. Some, you got the sense, were happy to see Twain's genius recognized in a way that it was not in his lifetime. He was certainly a popular author and wealthy beyond what anyone could have imagined. Yet there didn't seem to be a truly sincere appreciation of him as a literary giant at the time of his death. That may be why the eulogy of his friend, William Dean Howells rings so powerfully:

"Emerson, Longfellow, Lowell, Holmes—I knew them all—sages, poets, seers, critics, humorists; they were like one another and like other literary men; but Clemens was sole, incomparable, the Lincoln of our literature." In reading these pieces, you get the sense that these critics were just coming to grips with Twain's true place in our nation's literary heritage, especially after seeing Hemingway, Fitzgerald and other writers who followed Twain's lead.

Some of them, however, write with such arrogance, it can be a little tough to swallow. Marx, for example, seemed to be looking down on his readers, Twain and just about everybody else: "At this point, Clemens, only half escaped the genteel tradition, one of whose pre-eminent characteristics was an optimism undaunted by disheartening truth, returned to it. *Why* he did so is another story, having to do with his parents and his boyhood, with his own personality and his wife's and especially with the character of his audience. But whatever the explanation, the faint-hearted ending of *The Adventures of Huckleberry Finn* remains an important datum in the record of American thought and imagination. It has been noted before, both by critics, and nonprofessional readers. It should not be forgotten now." He goes on, "To minimize the seriousness of what must be accounted a major flaw in so great a work is, in a sense, to repeat Clemens' failure of nerve. This is disservice to criticism..." Couldn't have said it better myself.

Levy, Andrew. *Huck Finn's America.* New York: Simon & Schuster, 2015.

Andrew Levy's book on the America that greeted and genuinely seemed to misunderstand Twain's classic is well worth reading and an interesting new take on what Twain was trying to do with the novel. Levy's contention is that rather than see the book as it is taught now—a moralistic saga on race relations—Twain may have intended it just as much about the borders between parents and children and children's inner lives. Levy's theory is that when Twain set aside the *Huck* manuscript the first time, around August of 1876, he began a journal called "A Record of the Small Foolishnesses of Susie and 'Bay' Clemens (Infants)" about his own children. Levy says he stopped in 1885, the year *Huck* was published.

Seen through this lens, Levy sees a real connection between Twain's own children and the behaviors Twain describes through his characters in the novel. It's an interesting idea, but perhaps a bit of a stretch. He also includes a detailed examination of Twain's lengthy "Twins Of Genius" book tour with George Washington Cable to promote *Huckleberry Finn*, reading excerpts (including the much-maligned ending) to rapturous audiences across America. Since book tours are common these days, it's interesting to see what Twain, always interested in promoting good sales of his books, was willing to do.

Levy also quotes extensively—and with some astonishment—from the critics of the day who mention the frequent use of the "N" word, but barely even notice race. As he mentions a Hartford Courant review, a town where Twain lived, for goodness sakes, a line about Huck that truly is confounding: "Most amusing," the Courant writes, "is the struggle Huck has with his conscience in regard to slavery." Amusing?

Levy also includes a story that I'd never read elsewhere, one that for me clinched Twain's genuine intentions in using the "N" word so frequently. To some people, Twain's use of the "N" word was just careless, something that wasn't a big deal in 1885 but is now, something he just didn't know or understand or worry too much about. Maybe I'm reading too much into this incident, but on page 134, Levy recounts a story of Twain "riding a train westward," when he hears something upsetting. Evidently a "small country boy" had used the "N" word in public within "easy hearing distance" of "a negro woman." That action brought strong derision from the author, who had used it so frequently in the novel he was then working on.

In a letter to his wife, Olivia, dated January 8, 1883, or two years before *Huck* was published, Twain says the "negro woman" had "more brains & breeding than 7 generations of that boy's family." To me, that says Twain knew exactly the impact that word would have and how, for so many years, white America used it with utterly no regard for its impact; he felt he needed to do something about it and make them face up to their own insensitivity. If Twain critics had perhaps read that quote and understood the socially unpopular sentiment behind it, perhaps then they would see Twain as the crusader that others do. Then again, probably not.

Neider, Charles, ed. *Life As I Find It: A Treasury of Mark Twain Rarities.* New York: Cooper Square, 2000.

Just an absolute gem of a book. Compiled by noted and sometimes controversial Twain scholar Charles Neider, *Life As I Find It* was first pub-

Suggested Reading and Viewing

lished in 1961. It's a collection of Twain's writing that is a little hard to find but very well worth it. In the process of becoming one of the first Mark Twain scholars, Neider had access to all sorts of Twain's writing as he compiled Twain's first autobiography.

In what must have been quite a treasure hunt, Neider found some absolute classics that you won't find anywhere else. Some of them are just hilarious. One of my favorites, "Private Habits of Horace Greeley," which I read for the first time here, is included in Appendix B at the end of the book. I use it every year. At the time he wrote it, Twain was just beginning to get recognized as an author. Greeley was one of several newspaper publishers who helped pay Twain's fare for the Old World Tour that became his first book, *Innocents Abroad*. So, you could say Greeley was his boss. Twain lays into him in such clever fashion, you imagine Greeley himself laughing along. I like to use it to introduce Twain's attitude towards, well, just about everything. And there's more...

Skim through these 90-plus, usually brief articles and you'll find yourself chuckling, sometimes marveling at what Twain could do. Another favorite of mine is "A Boston Girl," which was published anonymously in the *Atlantic Monthly* in 1880 but the sharp-eyed Neider tracked it down many years later. It's a brief story about a letter writer who wanted to pick a grammatical bone with Mr. Twain: "This note comes to me from the home of culture: Dear Mr. ——: Your writings interest me very much; but I cannot help wishing you would not place adverbs between the particle and verb in the Infinitive. For example: 'to *even* realize,' 'to *mysteriously* disappear' 'to *wholly* do away.' You should say, *even* to realize; to disappear mysteriously, etc. 'rose up' is another mistake—tautology, you know. Yours truly, A Boston Girl."

Think about that one. Mark Twain gets a fan letter correcting his *grammar*? What do you think he's going to do with this? I sat there for a moment, laughing to myself, wondering if she realized what she got herself into. I read on:

> I print the note just as it is written, for one or two reasons: (1.) It flatters a superstition of mine that a person may learn to excel only in such details of an art as take a particularly strong hold upon his native predilections or instincts. (2.) It flatters another superstition of mine that whilst all the details of that art may be of equal importance, *he* cannot be made to feel that it is so. Possibly he may be made to *see* it, through argument and illustration; but never very sharply, I think.

Suggested Reading and Viewing

> Now I have certain instincts, and I wholly lack certain others. (Is that "wholly" in the right place?) For instance, I am dead to adverbs; they cannot excite me. To misplace an adverb is a thing which I am able to do with frozen indifference; it can never give me a pang. But when my young lady puts no point after "Mr."; when she begins "adverb," "verb" and "particle" with the small letter, and aggrandizes "Infinitive" with a capital; and when she puts no comma after "to mysteriously disappear," etc., I am troubled; and when she begins a sentence with a small letter I even *suffer*. Or I suffer, *even*—I do not know which it is; but she will, because the adverb is in her line, whereas only those minor matters are in mine. Mark these prophetic words; though this young lady's grammar be as the drifted snow for purity, she will never, never learn to punctuate while she lives; this is her demon, the adverb is mine.... We all have our limitations in the matter of grammar, I suppose...

Twain goes on to talk about writing, Bret Harte and tautology. This may be a personal thing, but if you've ever spent time dealing with editors, particularly on the newspaper side, you'll be laughing all the way through this. Like an umpire and being a husband, editing is a thankless job, one where you're expected to start perfect and improve. I can recall many times, squabbling with an editor over the way they wanted to awkwardly re-write my sentence so it sounded better to them, no doubt a distant descendant of the Boston Girl.

There are other classic pieces in here. How about, oh, Twain on woman's suffrage—"It will never do to allow women to vote. It will never do to allow them to hold office. You know, and I know, that if they were granted these privileges there would be no more peace on earth..." Or, "The last words of great men (and women)." What a nifty idea. Twain picks some good ones: "...for instance, Ben Franklin. "What sort of tactics did Franklin pursue? He pondered over his last words for as much as two weeks, and then when the time came, he said "None but the brave deserve the fair," and died happy. He could not have said a sweeter thing if he had lived till he was an idiot.... Twain adds some women, too: "Joan of Arc said, 'Tramp, tramp, tramp the boys are marching.' Queen Elizabeth said, 'Oh, I would give my kingdom for one moment more—I have forgotten my last words.'" He even included Alexander the Great, who said, "Another of those Santa Cruz punches, if you please," and his friend H.G. (Horace Greeley), whose dying words were, according to Twain, "I desire, now, to say a few words on political economy." Heh, heh, heh.

Though the media circus in those days wasn't much, Twain antici-pated what was coming. When Charles Dickens up and died, Twain noti-

Suggested Reading and Viewing

fied the world of "The Approaching Epidemic"—media overload: "One calamity to which the death of Mr. Dickens dooms this country has not awakened the concern to which its gravity entitles it. We refer to the fact that the nation is to be lectured to death all next winter, by Tom, Dick and Harry, with poor lamented Dickens for pretext. All the vagabonds who can spell with afflict the people with 'readings' from Pickwick and Copperfield, and all the insignificants who have been ennobled by the notice of a great novelist or transfigured by his smile will make a marketable commodity of it now, and turn the sacred reminiscence to the practical use of procuring bread and butter." Amazing how he anticipated the autograph/memorabilia blitz. Like with this entry: "'Heart Treasures of Precious Moments with Literature's Departed Monach.' A lecture. By Miss Serena Amelia Tryphenia McSpadden who still wears, and will always wear, a glove upon the hand made sacred by the clasp of Dickens. Only Death shall remove it." He wrote this in 1870. Amazing how well he saw what was coming.

A fascinating addendum to this already impressive collection is a closing section of 20 different newspaper stories/interviews/profiles on Twain, including his momentous meeting with the great Rudyard Kipling, who puts quite an unusual spin on his article. A number of these are "Mark Twain Returns Home" or "Mark Twain Home in Good Humor" types of articles, where you can imagine some cub reporter greeting Twain as he got off the boat, firing a bunch of silly questions and Twain throwing out quip after quip. Reading through these, you can just imagine what a delightful talk show guest Twain would have been: "So what do you think about President Trump?" Think of the pause, the furrowed brow, and then the quip that would kill.

Mentioning these stories reminds me of the famous Twain article, "Encounter With An Interviewer," which is also something I've used in class. You can find that online pretty much anywhere. In it, Twain is greeted by a local interviewer who is not particularly up on his writing and asked him a series of questions that, if Twain answered in a straight fashion ("When did you first begin to write?") would be pretty boring. Twain plays with the interviewer with some utterly ridiculous (and quite funny) responses—Q: "'How old are you?' (Twain is in his 70's at the time) A: '19. In June.' Q: 'Whom do you consider the most remarkable man you ever met?' A: 'Oh, I suppose George Washington.' Q: 'George WASHINGTON? How could you have met George Washington if you're only 19 years old?' A: 'Well, if you know more about me than I do why do you ask me?'" It goes from there. Very entertaining. I liked to use it in journalism classes. When we initially read it, some of the students thought Twain was rude and kind of cruel to the young writer, giving such silly answers. But, on further examination, I asked them to imagine writing a story for their newspaper with standard answers from Twain to such mundane questions: "How old are you? When did you first begin to write?" What Twain ended up doing is giving that cub reporter a story that nobody could have expected. It was really a gift.

This collection is highly recommended. And the story of Neider himself is interesting. Born in Russia, he became a writer and editor of some note in America, compiling Mark Twain's first autobiography, which, interestingly enough, drew harsh criticism from the Soviet Union in 1960, more or less at the height of the Cold War. The Soviets thought that Neider had censored (more or less) Twain's more critical views of the United States, something that Soviet readers, evidently, found entertaining. Neider, not a man to suffer this sort of insult from his native country, wrote back to then-Premier Nikita Khrushchev, asking for a chance to defend his decision. Khrushchev, amazingly, agreed, and Neider sent a 1,100-word reply, according to *The New York Times*. Great term paper topic, no?

Powers, Ron. *Mark Twain: A Life.* New York: Free Press, 2005.

Ron Powers' biography of Mark Twain was well received by just about everybody. It's long and quite well detailed and gives the reader a strong narrative of the many twists and turns of Twain's unusual life. The commentaries on his writing are good and thoughtful, and if you're a biography fan, it's well worth your time. There are pieces of Twain's that I would have liked to have more background on—"An Interesting Article," for example, or "Cooper's Literary Offenses," which gets just a paragraph. Later, Powers talks about Twain's relationship with Brander Matthews, then a prominent literary critic whose somewhat purple prose about Cooper and "the delicate art of the forest" are held up for lampooning by Twain.

Powers has a real feel for Twain and his work. As a review in the Guardian said, "The special joy of Ron Powers' Twain is not just that it's comprehensive but also that it places this great novel and its author in their proper historical context, and shows how life and work played against each other. Critical commentary on *Huckleberry Finn* is a sub-genre of American letters, and so is biographical analysis of Clemens/Twain. In this essential life, the two are brought together with an authority and understanding that is rare. Powers' sympathy for his subject also informs his account of Twain's final years, which are as grim as any in American literature." Indeed, having read so much about Twain's later years and the death of literally everyone around him, it amazes you that his writing continues to have the spark, the humor, and the intensity that it does right until the end.

Twain, Mark. *Adventures of Huckleberry Finn.* 125th anniversary ed. Edited by Victor Fischer, Lin Salamo, Harriett Elinor Smith, and Walter Blair. Berkeley: University of California Press, 2010.

Another worthwhile addition to the ever-growing *Huck Finn* library. This edition offers an assortment of different material as well as all of the original illustrations for Twain's initial publication. While I've never actually done this assignment, maybe I will if I ever get a chance to teach *Huck* again: ask your students to draw their version of Huck Finn, then compare it to the one Twain approved to appear in his actual book. It would be interesting to see what the students imagined vs. the illustrations Twain approved. As George Saunders notes in his "United States of Huck," there were some issues with the original illustrations, so you have to imagine that Twain was quite fed up with all the issues that seemed to go along with this publication. And they've never stopped.

There were many things I liked about this edition. It opens with several photographs and reproductions from the flyers for Twain and Cable's "Twins of Genius" tour, listing the readings that each speaker would give, some interesting letters from Twain to his wife while on tour. The one I liked was one he wrote around Thanksgiving in 1884 after a show at the Brooklyn Academy of Music. Twain writes, "Disposed of two great chops, 3 eggs, fried potatoes & a bottle of ale. I eat a big breakfast every morning, & a big supper every night & am growing fat." Later, in Canada, he keeps going: "he ate a hearty breakfast at 9 this morning. On the hotel car at 1 p.m, I took a sirloin steak & mushrooms, sweet potatoes, Irish ditto, plate of trout, bowl of tomato soup, 3 cups of coffee, 4 pieces of apple pie (or one complete pie), 2 plates of ice cream & 1 orange. But I stopped then,

Suggested Reading and Viewing

on account of the expense, though still hungry." I don't know about your eating habits, but that is one amazing meal. Maybe I might have had a run at it when I was 18, but that's a lot of food. Twain must have had an amazing metabolism.

Next up is a collection of maps of the area, something I found useful to show the class exactly Huck and Jim's route down the Mississippi. This also gave me the idea for one of the project-based learning assignments, suggesting that Huck, just for the heck of it, decides to send postcards back to Tom Sawyer from all of his stops and adventures along the way. (Of course, he wouldn't really have done that, since he was supposed to be dead ... but it made for a fun project.) I had one marvelous student who hand-drew about 10 postcards that were beautifully done.

Following the maps are about 75 pages of explanatory notes to go along with Twain's text and they are fascinating. For example, when Pap is described as "a father ... lay drunk with the hogs in the tanyard) the explanatory note says The chief model for Pap Finn was the Hannibal town drunkard Jimmy Finn, although Pap may owe something to 'General' Gaines and Woodson Blankenship; his bellicosity when drunk to Gaines, and his fatherhood to Blankenship.... Mark Twain wrote at least five separate descriptions of Jimmy Finn..." Well, you get the point. Very detailed and informative.

From a teaching perspective, the next section—"Three Passages from the Manuscript"—is a wonderful tool. If you've ever had any experience at all teaching high school students, one of their major objections to any sort of writing assignment is the re-write. If you're in the writing business, you understand that's a part of it. But in school, that doesn't happen very often.

I remember once editing, crossing out things, and generally marking up a student's paper at my desk—she sat in front so she could see me do it—and she was visibly distressed: "What are you doing to my paper? What are you doing to my paper?" she shouted, coming up to my desk as if to take it away. "I'm editing your paper," I explained. "Trying to make it better." Not every student buys into the fact that you can almost always make a piece of writing better—if you work at it. One exercise I've done in class is to print out the two versions of the manuscript, with his editing and written-in additions, then go through it, line by line. Almost always, the students are amazed at how carefully, how well crafted each sentence actually is. The idea, of course, is to try to get them to model that in their own writing, which, of course, doesn't always work. Worth a try, though.

Suggested Reading and Viewing

In Ken Burns' terrific two-part *Mark Twain* series, a clip from playwright Arthur Miller testifies to Twain's fine-tuning of his own work: "He was chiseling it out," he said, "He made it seem like an effusion, like it was dripping off him like a shower-bath. But you read any page of his and you know that there's a poet, crafting all those lines. It's hard to improve on any of his lines." Burns' series then shows a few of Twain's manuscript pages with all the cross-outs and additions. You can see that these pages were labored over. To some of my students, who never felt when reading the book that there was that kind of intensive labor behind it, it was revelatory.

One feature that was interesting in the 125th edition were some Twain re-writes of chapter nineteen, some lovely descriptions of the river and happy times with Jim. Comparing the first version with the rewritten, final version, you can see Twain paring the language down, smoothing out the narrative. It was instructive to share a couple of these pages with my students, showing how he edited his own work, took out some unnecessary phrases, and added words where he needed them so they noticed that to a real craftsman, a real writer, the work is never done. I explained to them that in my newspaper days and even writing books, there probably isn't a writer in the world who, when he was finished, would admit he was finished. They almost always want to go back, add a little, and tinker a bit. (Same goes here.)

What was neat, and the students got a big kick out of this, is that they included a handful of photographs of Twain's actual manuscript, including an actually drawn-to-scale title page, which read, *Adventures of Huckleberry Finn (in small print) Tom Sawyer's Comrade* By Mark Twain New York Chas. L. Webster 1885."

For many of my students, seeing the actual, handwritten manuscript brought a strong response, as if, for perhaps the first time, they recognized the human being behind this book, that someone had to sit down with a pen and a piece of paper and write this down.

Twain, Mark. *Adventures of Huckleberry Finn*. New York: Signet Classics, 2008.

The Signet Classics edition of *Adventures of Huckleberry Finn* to me was a godsend. I was able to obtain a classroom set of this paperback version through our book buyer in a trade for a hardbound edition of *Jane Eyre*. (I got a classroom set of *Walden* and *Dubliners* and this. No baseball

Suggested Reading and Viewing

GM ever did better; nobody at my school was reading *Jane Eyre*.) The revelation for me was Phillips' afterword, which, remarkably, was the one piece I've read since I started working on this project that defended Twain's ending and to her, sealed up the book perfectly. Reading it the first time, I wasn't sure I was reading it correctly, so I stopped and went back. And it's made more and more sense to me every time I've read it since. She begins by asking a good question: "Is there any earthly reason for an afterword, an 'epilogue or commentary on literary work' to *Adventures of Huckleberry Finn*?" And she goes on to demonstrate convincingly—to me, at least—that there indeed is, if you have something new to say. She does:

> Having won an audience with the book's precursor, the relatively benign The Adventures Of Tom Sawyer (Twain himself called the book "simply a hymn to boyhood") Twain uses the scrim of another rootin'-tootin' adventure yard to pursue a very different agenda. Though he provides the classic qualifications of rite-of-passage adventure—orphans alone in the world, bands of boys, murder and mayhem, the raft on the River—Twain wields Huck's seamless, silken vernacular like a samurai magician, seducing his largely racist readership into empathizing with a runaway slave, and then (to skewer more progressive readers equally) participating in the sadistic humiliation of a slave who is no longer a slave. Twain, a white man and a satirist, did not think highly of white men and their kingdoms. He pulls the moral rug from under the reader repeatedly before the reader knows he's standing on it.

Well, when I read that, I just thought, wow. That might well be it. Then, she went on to explain the ending, as she saw it:

> How dark is dark? Critics from Hemingway to Doctorow have questioned the resolution of *Huckleberry Finn*, when Tom Sawyer appears and takes charge of the plot, as a failure of nerve (right, Leo?) or inspiration. Not so, Reader. Here the novel comes full circle, still bitterly "funny," more and more savage, into Twain's own "heart of darkness." The charming Tom "respectable and well brung up; and had a character to lose, becomes "Mars Tom," who manipulates Jim and co-opts Huck for his own entertainment, then pays Jim forty dollars for his time. Jim has saved his life; no matter. Tom Sawyer, friends and co-conspirator, innocent as a mint julep or magnolia blossom, is evil come to life, unforgiveable, unredeemable, unto the next generation.

Now, how does that sit with you? Impressive, isn't it? And knowing that Twain would go on to write many pieces protesting American intervention and Imperialist behavior overseas, Phillips sees this ending as foreshadowing that turn of mind for Twain.

For when Aunt Polly innocently—and logically—asks why, if Jim was already free, they put him through all that, Tom's nasty response echoes something we might have seen tweeted in recent months: "Just like women! Why, I wanted *adventure* of it; and I'd a waded neck deep in blood to –" His chilling comment, undercut by the sudden appearance of patient Aunt Polly, calls to mind the 'adventures' of war and colonialism, and the hundreds of thousands sacrificed to the ambitious, wrongheaded schemes of 'leaders.' Tom Sawyer, beloved representative of horror, a blond Kurtz recovering in a feather bed." For me, this hit home in a powerful way. And if she's right, if that was Twain's intent, well, how prescient and on-target was he? Is that where America was/is headed? Suddenly, a boy's book becomes so very much more.

Twain, Mark. *The Adventures of Huckleberry Finn*. Norton Critical Edition, 3d ed. Edited by Thomas Cooley. New York: W.W. Norton, 1999.

This third Norton Critical Edition, edited by Thomas Cooley from Ohio State, is terrific, and gives in one place all sorts of cool supplemental items in addition to Twain's text. While there are many good editions out there, if I had to give the Mr. Nogo Seal of Approval to one, it'd be this one. Not only does it include the entire text of the novel with some excellent footnotes, there is a terrific assemblage of supplemental material to help you teach the novel as deeply as you want to go.

For example, if you're teaching poetry and want a good laugh and would like to see Twain's models for the horrible Emmeline Grangerford's morbid poetry, there are several examples of similar work from that exact time period. There are also a number of excerpts from Twain's letters discussing the writing of *Huck Finn* and his great relief when it was finished. "The sight of a proof-slip is always exasperating to me"; Twain wrote to William Dean Howells, who had evidently agreed to help out his frustrated friend by reading some of the proofs: "...on this book," Twain confesses, "it was maddening."

The third edition also includes several early reviews, including one from the aforementioned Brander Matthews—he of the "Cooper's delicate art of the forest"—and some critical reviews of the book. It also includes a rare item: After *Huck* started to draw criticism from some editorial board, Twain decided to include a response to them. Titled "Twain's Replies to the Newspapers" it's maybe our first tweet: "Huckleberry Finn is not an imaginary person. He still lives; or rather, *they* still live; for Huckleberry

Suggested Reading and Viewing

Finn is two persons in one—namely, the author's two uncles, the present editors of the Boston *Advertiser* and the Springfield *Republican*. In character, language, clothing, education, instinct, and origin, he is the painstakingly and truthfully draw photograph and counterpart of these two gentlemen as they were in the time of their boyhood, forty years ago. The work has been more carefully and conscientiously done, and is exactly true to the originals, in even the minutest particulars, with but one exception, and that trifling one; this boy's language has been toned down and softened, here and there, in deference to the taste of a more modern and fastidious day." Unfortunately, the idea was nixed by the always-cautious Olivia Clemens, but the idea is precious.

Twain was able, evidently, to get off one response, this one to the *Omaha World-Herald*, on my birthday (August 23) a few years before I arrived (1902):

> Your telegram has arrived, but I have already said all I want to say concerning Huck Finn's new adventures; there is no need to say it over again.... I am fearfully afraid this noise is doing much harm. It has started a number of hitherto spotless people to reading *Huck Finn*, out of natural human curiosity to learn what this is all about—people who had not heard of him before; people whose morals will go to rack and ruin now.
>
> The publishers are glad; but it makes me want to borrow a handkerchief and cry. I should be sorry to think it was the publishers themselves that got up this entire little flutter to enable them to unload a book that was taking too much room in their cellars, but you can never tell what a publisher will do. I have been one myself.

Right underneath Twain's letter is, of course, a burst of invective from *Huck* critic John Wallace (wouldn't be right to leave him out). It begins so subtly, you wonder how long he studied over his opening line: "*Adventures of Huckleberry Finn* by Mark Twain, is the most grotesque example of racist trash ever written..."

What also makes it a great buy is also the criticism, which includes Jane Smiley's "Say It Ain't So, Huck," which, I think, will get your students stirred up after reading the book. It did me. Lastly, it also includes another famous female novelist's take on the book. Toni Morrison's "This Amazing, Troubling Book" is an intelligent and thoughtful way to look at what Twain was *trying* to do, swimming against the political current of the time. And for $12.50, it's a real bargain.

Index

administrator response to *Huckleberry Finn* 74–78
The Adventures of Huckleberry Finn 1,2, 4, 5, 10, 12, 13, 14, 16, 17, 18, 21, 22, 23, 29, 32, 39, 68, 74, 80, 85, 87, 88, 90, 92, 93, 95, 98, 100, 101; criticism of 20, 70, 71; humor in 28, 57; intelligence of 28, 66; multiple themes in 23–29, 66, 68; process of writing 38; religion in 25–26, 29, 57–58; response to Huck's prank 2–33–34; superstitions in 27; transformative qualities of 60; writing of 15
The Adventures of Tom Sawyer 73, 86, 92, 116, 135
African Americans 1, 5, 17, 19, 35, 36
apology, classroom reaction to Huck's 35
Asch, Solomon 102
The Atlantic 125

Banks, Russell 50
Bellow, Saul 99
Beloved 77
Black Lives Matter movement 17
Blount, Roy, Jr. 29, 71
Boston Advertiser 125
Bourne, Jason 58
Bradley, David 19, 62
The Braindead Microphone 12
Burns, Ken 14, 19, 38, 50, 154–155
Burr, Aaron 112, 114, 115

Carver, Raymond 99
Cask of Amontillado 7
Catch 22 68
Chadwick, Jocelyn 19
Chekhov, Anton 85, 98
The Cincinnati Enquirer 133–135
Civil War 6, 34
Civitello, Mary Ann 9

Clemens, Clara 15
Clemens, Livy 15
Clemens, Samuel 8, 9, 11
Clemens, Susy 15
Coca-Cola 3, 98
code-switching in *Huckleberry Finn* 55
The College Board 74, 75, 76
Collins, Wilkie 136
Common Core 69
compassion 57–58
Concord 6, 20
Concord Public Library 20
Confederate Army 72
A Connecticut Yankee In King Arthur's Court 8, 64
Cooper, James Fenimore 53, 92
Cooper's Literary Offenses 11, 135–149
Cratchit, Bob 88
The Crucible 3
Cunningham, Sam 10

Dallas 10
Danby, Major 68
The Deerslayer, analysis of 135–143
description, use of 41
DeVoto, Bernard 62, 91
dialect, use of 31, 33
Dickens, Charles 7, 85
Doctorow, E.L. 64
Dostoevsky, Fyodor 88
Douglass, Frederick 16, 97

East Gadsden High School 2
Ebert, Roger 53
Eliot, T.S. 70, 99, 100–101
Elizabeth, sharing story of 44
Ellison, Ralph 99
Emancipation Proclamation 34
Emerson, Ralph Waldo 87

170 Index

An Encounter with an Interviewer 11, 110–116
ending 10, 53, 60, 69, 90
An Entertaining Article 11, 125–135
Everest, Mount 68

Faulkner, William 99
The Federalist Papers 9
Ferguson, MO 10
Fiedler, Leslie 70
Finch, Atticus 77, 79
Fisher Fishkin, Shelly 19
Fitzgerald, F. Scott 4, 87
Florida 6, 9
Florida Department of Education 4
Foote, Shelby 71
Fortunato 7
Francoeur, Sister Marjorie 8

The Galaxy 130
Geismar, Maxwell 155
Gettysburg 117, 119
Gillespie, Mike 9
Gogol, Nikolai 85
Grangerford, Buck 39
Grangerford, Emmeline 39, 40
Grant, Ulysses 116
"Great Books" 16
The Great Gatsby 3, 10
Greeley, Horace 105–110

Hamilton, Alexander 9
Hamlet 9, 40, 42, 80
Harpers 30, 69, 70, 71, 101
Hawthorne, Nathaniel 7, 91
Hayes, Rutherford B. 116
Heller, Joseph 68
Hemingway, Ernest 11, 52, 62, 64, 74, 91, 99
heroism 58
Holbrook, Hal 18, 19, 28, 30, 39, 43, 110, 115, 155–156
How I Edited an Agricultural Paper 11, 119–126
Howells, William Dean 8, 9, 22, 85, 125
Huck Finn's America 20, 157–158

Ice Cube 16
Innocents Abroad 116, 125–135
"Is Huckleberry Finn's Ending Really Lacking?" 100–104
Ivy League 1

Jefferson, Thomas 9
Jenner, Kendall 17
Jim 11, 12, 16, 21, 27, 31, 32, 33, 34, 35, 40, 48, 52, 56, 58, 62, 63, 65, 76, 77, 89, 91, 92, 97, 103
Joyce, James 9

Kaplan, Justin 72
Kelly, George 103
King Lear 90
King Solomon 32
Konnikova, Maria 11, 12, 58, 60, 62, 63, 94, 100
Krutch, Joseph Wood 70
Kurtz (*Heart of Darkness*) 64

Lee, Harper 4
Letterman, David 138
Lettis, Richard 156
Levy, Andrew 20, 157–158
Life on the Mississippi 39, 135
Lincoln's Gettysburg Address 69
Little House on the Prairie 72
Loftus, Judith, Mrs. 32
The London Saturday Review 130–135
Lounsbury, Professor Thomas 136

Macbeth 7
Maher, Bill 16, 100
Mailer, Norman 70
Marianna Trench 4
Marionettes, Inc. 46
Mark Twain Tonight 18, 28, 35, 43, 73
Marx, Leo 12, 27, 62, 63, 69, 91, 101, 103
Maryland 10
Mason-Dixon Line 19
Matthews, Brander 136, 147–149
Melville, Herman 7, 9, 91
Michigan 6, 9
Minnesota 10, 43
Mississippi River 27, 32, 33, 42, 65, 70, 83, 103
Missouri 43
moment of truth 49–50
Monty Python 23, 110
moral code 46, 47, 48–49
Morrison, Toni 81, 99
Mount Everest 68
murder, student response to 40

The "N" word 5, 15–22
Napoleon 62, 91
Neider, Charles 158–162
New York Evening Post 116–117
New York Times 70
New York Times Book Review 70
Night 10

"Pap" 18, 19, 27, 32, 47, 59
Partisan Review 70

The Pathfinder, analysis of 144
Pennsylvania 10
Pettit, Arthur 96
Phelps' farm 11, 48, 55, 70
Phillips, Jayne Ann 64
Poe, Edgar Allen 7
Potter, Harry 54
Powell, Dawn 71
Powers, Ron 162–163
A Presidential Candidate 11, 116–119
Pride and Prejudice 10
Private Habits of Horace Greeley 11, 105–110
Pudd'n'head Wilson 73

Quarry Farm 14

racial attitude 27, 35, 50; Southern 19, 35–36
A Raisin in the Sun 3
The Ray Bradbury Theater 46
Rivier College 8
Romeo and Juliet 7, 84
Roskelly, Hepsibah 79, 80

Salinger, J.D. 99
Salon 3
Santayana, George 94–95
Sasse, Ben 16
The Saturday Review 126, 130
Saunders, George 12, 13, 30, 39, 53, 62, 64
Sawyer, Tom 11, 12, 21, 25, 27, 31, 52, 56, 57, 58, 59, 60, 62, 63, 65, 71, 79, 81, 86, 101, 102
Say It Ain't So, Huck 30, 69
The Scarlet Letter 10
The Scientific American 11, 62, 94, 100
Scotland Yard 23
Scott, Sir Walter 11, 13, 32, 58
Scrooge 84
Seinfeld finale 47
Shakespeare, William 7, 42

Shepherson, Sophia 40
Sherburn, Colonel 43
slavery 6, 16, 63
Smiley, Jane 1, 29, 30, 58, 63, 69, 70, 71, 101, 104
Springfield Republican 20
Stewart, Jon 138
Stowe, Harriet Beecher 16
Styron, William 71, 72

Tallahassee Community College 9
Their Eyes Were Watching God 77
Thoreau, Henry 6, 20
To Kill a Mockingbird 3, 4, 7
Tom and Huck, differences between 12–13, 93–96
Trilling, Lionel 70, 89, 100, 101
Trump, Donald 16, 64, 65
Trump, Donald, Jr. 117
Twain, Mark 1,2, 4, 6, 7, 8, 9, 10, 11, 13, 14, 17, 23, 26, 27, 30–32, 39, 47, 65, 71, 74, 90–98
Twain/Holbrook: An American Odyssey 73
Twain-related assignments 150–153
Twins of Genius Tour 32, 158–159

Ulysses 9
Uncle Tom's Cabin 71, 72, 73
The United States of Huck 12, 20, 22, 83–99

Virginia 10

Wallace, John 16–17, 58
Washington, Booker T. 97
Washington, George 113, 117
Waterloo 62, 91
Watson, Miss 25–26, 49, 74, 94
Whitman, Walt 87

Yossarian 68
YouTube 16, 18

www.ingramcontent.com/pod-product-compliance
Ingram Content Group UK Ltd.
Pitfield, Milton Keynes, MK11 3LW, UK
UKHW042016140426
5217IPUK00015B/1201